Careers in Asset Management and Retail Brokerage

2006 Edition

WetFeet Insider Guide

WetFeet®

Helping you make smarter career decisions.

WetFeet, Inc.

The Folger Building
101 Howard Street
Suite 300
San Francisco, CA 94105

Phone: (415) 284-7900 or 1-800-926-4JOB
Fax: (415) 284-7910
Website: www.WetFeet.com

Careers in Asset Management and Retail Brokerage

2006 Edition
ISBN: 1-58207-517-4

Table of Contents

Asset Management and Retail Brokerage at a Glance

Opportunity Overview

- Undergrads from all majors are recruited to work in operations, research, trading, customer service, marketing, and sales. Positions with direct customer contact usually require licenses. Undergrads are rarely accepted into retail brokerage training programs, which are usually reserved for midcareer professionals.

- Hot talent right out of business school may come in as portfolio managers, but more likely they will start as assistant managers, researchers, and analysts, providing support and resources for decision-makers. Some eventually become fund managers. Retail brokerage jobs also require relevant real-world experience.

- Midcareer professionals with experience in direct mail, advertising, bank operations, communications, data processing, retailing, and other customer service industries can find midlevel jobs at mutual funds and other asset management companies. Retail brokerage houses will consider midcareer professionals as brokers, usually in their 30s to early 40s, with proven success in other fields.

Major Pluses about Careers in This Industry

- Generous compensation.

- High visibility, particularly for fund managers.

- Dynamic environment that changes with daily market fluctuations.

- Merit-based: If you're good at making money for investors, you can make lots yourself.

- The satisfaction of helping people achieve financial security.

- Excellent benefits and vacation packages.

- Abundant holidays, compliments of the New York Stock Exchange.

- Management ranks are ripe for a shift as Baby Boomer senior execs get ready to take their bull market winnings and retire.

Major Minuses about Careers in This Industry

- Vulnerability to business and stock market cycles.

- Increased regulations in the wake of trading scandals make day-to-day work more complicated at the very least.

- Highly structured environment in larger firms makes it easy to feel slotted or pigeonholed.

- Grueling hours in the retail brokerage industry.

- As long as your clients' money is in the market, you're working—regardless of vacations, sick days, or your best friend's wedding.

Recruiting Overview

- The recruiting process is formal and highly competitive for portfolio managers and the analyst jobs that lead up to them. It's less formal but still very selective for other positions.

- A variety of channels to jobs in the industry are available, from campus recruiting for analysts and private client positions, to job searches through the Internet or via headhunters. Networking is usually the key to finding a job at a hedge fund.

- The industry is still pulling out of the slump caused by the twin blows of a bear market and scandal. Recruiters are hiring, albeit at a guarded pace.

- Brokerage training programs at top-tier firms are often closed to most undergrads and MBAs. Midcareer professionals with solid experience and contacts have a better chance of securing a place in a training program.

- Candidates with top-shelf analytical skills accompanied by technical skills are in demand.

- The industry seeks out non-MBA graduate degree holders, especially those with math, statistics, and physics PhDs, for positions as quantitative analysts.

- The hedge fund sector has grown rapidly, driven by outsized performance gains. Competition for these spots is fierce, even as returns appear to slow.

The Industries

Overview

"Because that's where the money is." Willy Sutton's immortal reply to the reporter who asked him why he robbed banks might also explain why people go into the asset management and retail brokerage industries. Indeed, companies such as State Street Global and Barclays Global Investors had over a trillion dollars in assets under management at the beginning of 2005; a host of other money managers are nipping at the heels of these two. Asset management and retail brokerage firms are in the business of using money to make more of it. In the process, many people who work in the industry have made a lot of it for themselves, too. Moreover, though they have done it with hard work and intensity, many people in the industry have successfully avoided the death-march common in investment banking and management consulting.

Asset management companies manage the money of their clients to achieve specific financial objectives within guidelines under which the investment pool is organized. The pool might take the form of a mutual fund, hedge fund, retirement or pension fund, or other institutional fund and, depending on how the fund is organized, could invest in any range of investment vehicles including equities, fixed-income securities, and derivative products. As a retail stockbroker or financial advisor, you provide much the same function as asset managers: picking stocks, determining the right portfolio mix, executing trades, and ultimately increasing or preserving wealth—albeit on a smaller scale and with fewer investment tools at your disposal—for individual investors. The asset management juggernaut requires an equally enormous infrastructure. For every fund, there is not only a fund manager, but also a team of analysts to research equities and fixed-income investments, economists and other soothsayers to augur the direction of the market and economy, salespeople and marketers to get people to buy the fund, traders to execute orders, accountants to track assets, and legions of tech specialists and back-office staff. There's a similar infrastructure for retail brokerages. Ultimately, all these people are trying to make money for their clients and themselves.

Anyone considering a career in asset management should be keenly aware that markets not only go up, but also go down—sometimes way down. There was a time, in another century, when the markets were on a rocket ship to the moon. The year was 1999 and the entire financial industry was, well, partying like it was 1999. Suburbanites dropping the kids off to school in their Dodge Caravans spoke about stocks with a passion they had hitherto reserved for Oprah's Book Club selections. Everyone was a financial genius—not just brokers and fund managers, but secretaries and butchers. Even pimply-faced kids in junior high were expert stock pickers.

The hangover from all that partying made the financial services industry a much more sober place. The rookies were largely sidelined, and investments became once again the bailiwick of professionals. The stock market made a comeback in 2003, with the Nasdaq rebounding 50 percent by year-end and the S&P 500 gaining 26 percent. Despite a fourth quarter rally, 2004 showed more modest growth. Still, investors showed that the bear market during the first part of the decade hadn't turned them off stocks altogether—just that they wanted indexes to point north before they plunked down their cash. Stock-based mutual funds took in $177.5 billion in net assets in 2004, up 17 percent from the previous year and the largest annual inflow since 2000, says the Investment Company Institute (ICI). Meanwhile, the biggest firms have been gaining a larger piece of the investing pie: The top ten firms captured an estimated 90 percent of the industry's total net inflow in 2004.

Hiring didn't track the indexes point for point, as a mutual fund trading scandal caused several firms to batten down the hatches and review piles of e-mails and trades, and eventually make big settlements with regulators. Executive search firm Russell Reynolds estimates that overall hiring of retail mutual fund portfolio managers slowed in 2004. Perhaps not surprisingly, compliance officers and related functions skirted that trend

INSIDER TIP

The industry may never again see the growth in client assets and hiring that it did in the 1990s. But the biggest firms continue to cull the best and brightest from the year's graduating class, and some expect firms will take on more staff in 2005–06 than the year earlier.

and saw their demand and compensation increase. And in keeping with the industry's deepening love affair with their wealthiest clients, compensation and demand for wealth managers and hedge fund professionals also gained on that of past years. For brokerages, hiring inched up 2 percent from the prior year, estimates the Securities Industry Association.

Amidst the broken chandeliers and shattered vases of the postbubble financial industry, some potentially exceptional opportunities still exist. "I'd expect growth in the industry to be as fast or faster than employment growth in the general economy," says one recruiter. And if you do manage to find (and keep) a job in the industry, you can still expect to make a solid living and retain something of a life, particularly compared to the slave-labor existence of your investment banking peers.

The Bottom Line

With the tremendous proliferation of 401(k), IRA, and other types of retirement plans during the 1990s, more people than ever before can now be classified as investors. An estimated 92 million individuals in 54 million households, or nearly half of all U.S. households, owned mutual funds in 2004, says the ICI. The choices for the small-time investor have never been greater, including stocks, bonds, mutual funds, real estate trusts, exchange-traded funds (ETFs), and options. There's also a range of venues available should one have an itch to invest, including traditional full-service firms, discount brokerages, and do-it-yourself online trading. And we haven't even considered the institutional investor yet. The pensions, insurance companies, corporations, foundations, and endowments that used to comprise nearly all investors are still around, and money managers are still there to try to create wealth for them.

This all boils down to a wide range of career options in a dynamic industry. What's in demand is closely tied to a firm's strategy. Discount brokers, the ones that benefited the most from average Joe day-trading, have kept a tight cap on headcount now that Joe has gone back to his day job. The largest, generally New York–based, brokerage houses (sometimes called *wirehouses*) continue to recruit trainees for number-crunching analyst positions and more sales-oriented marketing and brokerage support jobs. And the merger frenzy that took hold of the financial services sector in the late 1990s and early part of this decade has endowed some regional players with bigger aspirations. Wachovia Securities, for instance, is planning to ramp up its brokerage operation and start a new broker-in-training program over the next year.

Industry Breakdown

Asset management companies and retail brokerages occupy only a part of the matrix that is the financial services industry. Nevertheless, it's worth looking at the industry as a whole for a few reasons. First, it's helpful to know what retail brokerages and asset management firms are *not*. Next, the boundaries between different sectors in the industry often blur, with firms in one sector participating in the activities of another. Finally, as the industry goes through its current consolidation phase, firms that once occupied different places in the landscape now find themselves under the same roof.

Many leading full-service financial institutions now have investment banking and retail brokerage arms. Citigroup became a top-tier investment banking player when it merged with Travelers and its Salomon Smith Barney subsidiary back in 1998, Chase when it acquired J.P. Morgan in 2000. Investment bankers essentially help corporations issue debt or equity securities. The obvious example is the investment bank that underwrites an initial public offering (IPO) for a start-up firm. But investment bankers don't stop when the IPOs dry up; they also advise companies on M&A targets, find companies buyers, and help companies meet their capital needs by underwriting secondary public offerings and debt issuances. Investment bankers are the storks that deliver securities to markets.

Brokerages also typically have equity research units made up of analysts and their helpers, who research and recommend stocks to mostly institutional clients. Research drives trading volume and lends investment banks a sense of expertise and authority in the industries in which they specialize. Investment bankers are usually closely allied with capital markets units of major brokerage houses. Capital markets operations then make markets for the securities that have been issued; that is, they find buyers and sellers for newly issued securities. Capital markets departments typically house a brokerage firm's stock and bond traders. These in turn might sell to any number of other traders who represent retail brokerages, mutual funds, or other institutional investors. Linking up these buyers and sellers are brokers.

Brokerage houses often have retail operations that allow individual investors to buy and sell stocks, bonds, and mutual funds. More often than not, they also have private banking operations that cater to wealthy individuals. Then there are the institutional investors—the asset managers, pension fund managers, and mutual fund managers who invest assets on behalf of their clients. Institutional clients include government or private pension funds, corporate retirement plans, or insurance companies. Alongside these primary functions are a number of support roles, including marketing and sales, back-office operations, and compliance, that, although less glamorous, are no less important to the frictionless turning of the industry.

ASSET MANAGEMENT COMPANIES

Asset managers, also called *investment managers* or *money managers*, are responsible for investing the assets of a group, institution, or individual according to specified management goals. Asset management companies are typically organized around funds and run by portfolio managers. These people have a coterie of analysts to support them. Unlike high-profile sell-side analysts, buy-side analysts—those that support managers—typically analyze a number of companies across industry groups and don't offer their research outside the company. Additionally, larger funds might have strategic analysts and economists on staff to help predict the market direction for a family of funds. Large money managers also employ traders to execute their purchases and sales of securities. Asset managers sometimes have back-office operations to process the settlement of orders. Finally, firms have sales and relationship management teams to get the general public or institutional investors to buy their asset management services.

Asset management breaks down into five major categories:

Mutual Fund Management

Mutual fund management includes funds raised with money from individual share-holders and institutions that invest in any combination of stocks, bonds, and money market instruments, according to very specific investment goals, and adhere to strict governance laws. Mutual funds are regulated under the Investment Company Act of 1940. True mutual funds are considered "open-ended"; that is, investors can buy or sell shares at any time based on the value of the assets at that time. Closely related to mutual funds are closed-end funds, which offer a fixed number of shares; ETFs, which trade on major exchanges; and unit investment trusts, which offer dividends or interest to their shareholders and have set termination dates.

Modern mutual funds got their American start in 1924 when George Putnam, of the eponymous firm, offered a diversified portfolio of stocks and bonds to the public. Mutual funds have become increasingly popular over the last 15 years, rising in number from 3,079 in 1990 to 8,046 at the end of 2004. Over the last few years, the rate of growth has slowed. In keeping with general industry sluggishness, fund firms launched just 260 funds in 2004, down from 300 in 2003, which was already less than in 2002, according to Morningstar. While the reigning champion of the mutual fund industry has been Fidelity Investments with $960 billion in assets under management, chal-lengers like second-ranked fund company, The Vanguard Group, and third-ranking American Funds (a subsidiary of The Capital Group) have been gaining ground on the Boston giant.

Retail Asset Management

Retail asset management includes a host of services, primarily for high-net-worth indi-viduals, that includes trusts and professionally managed accounts (you consent to leave the investment decisions to the professionals, much to the delight of trustafarians everywhere who can better spend their time on independent film projects or following

Green Day concerts). A client's net worth or level of investable assets usually determines the level of service he or she receives, from call center to personal banker. Those that cater to high-net-worth clients tend to offer more exotic investments, such as private equity funds, in part because they're not restricted by regulations designed to protect smaller nest eggs from risky investments. Unlike commission-based brokerage accounts, retail asset managers usually charge a fee based on a percentage of assets under management. Major brokerage houses, such as Merrill Lynch and Morgan Stanley, and many specialized asset management companies offer retail asset management services.

Hedge Fund Management

Much of the public perception of hedge funds is replete with images of elitist investment cabals domiciled on the Gold Coast of Connecticut that make their clients fabulously wealthy through Byzantine investment instruments—which is precisely what makes hedge funds so alluring. Because they work outside many of the SEC regulatory and reporting strictures that are imposed on mutual funds, hedge funds are often open only to institutional and accredited investors. The trend has been to democratize funds and some have lowered investment minimums to $25,000. These still have the same freedom to use instruments such as derivatives, leverage, and shorting. The latter, which is betting that a stock will go down, gives hedge funds an edge during a bear cycle. "Because they don't short, mutual funds are more exposed to the market's ups and downs," says one hedge fund employee.

Their flexibility translated into some hefty returns during the stock market's worse days. But the average performance has dimmed slightly over the past year, perhaps because there are more and more players having a go at the same game. "You have more people trying to do it—there's a natural bias toward mediocrity," says one industry observer. Last year, the Van Global Hedge Fund Index rose 8 percent, outpacing bond funds but short of the S&P 500's 11 percent gain. More modest returns haven't dissuaded wealthy individuals that hedge funds are the next best thing since Tiffany's small blue boxes: Hedge fund adviser the Hennessee Group estimates that assets in hedge funds rose 17 percent last year to $934 billion.

These investment vehicles are popular with their managers, too. In addition to a management fee based on a percentage of assets managed, fund managers receive enormous incentive compensation based on the (positive) returns of the fund. A fund manager typically receives a management fee of 1 to 2 percent of assets along with 20 percent of overall profits. This arrangement is called "one and twenty" in the industry. However, some funds have built-in clauses that ensure that they only pay out the percentage of profits for aggregate gains. That is, if a firm loses money one year, the manager doesn't see a percentage of profits until the fund's gains have surpassed its losses. In addition to fees and a percentage of profits, fund managers typically have their own money invested in these funds, which certainly allies their interests with those of their investors. Larger hedge fund companies include Pequot Capital Management, Tremont Capital Management (a subsidiary of OppenheimerFunds), and Andor Capital Management. Many leading brokerage firms and asset management companies also have these alternative investment products.

Institutional Asset Management

Institutional asset managers invest money on behalf of corporations, insurance companies, pension funds, endowments, and charitable foundations. Asset managers offer this wide range of clientele a picnic basket full of investment goodies, including money market funds, equity investments, fixed-income products, 401(k) administration, and active and indexed funds.

Pension and Retirement Fund Management

Pension and retirement fund management is exactly as the name implies. Back in the good old days when workers didn't have to fund their own retirement plans through 401(k)s and IRAs, employers used to set money aside for their employees' retirement. Ah, how times have changed. Nevertheless, pension funds do exist; the largest of these, the California Public Employees' Retirement System (a.k.a. CalPERS), has $185 billion in assets. As you might guess, the most populous states in the union have the largest employee retirement funds; following CalPERS are the California State Teachers'

Retirement System ($126 billion) and the New York State Common Retirement Fund ($119 billion). The largest private pension plan is that of General Motors, with $91 billion in assets. Pension plans either invest assets themselves or rely on an institutional advisor to invest for them.

RETAIL BROKERAGES

Retail brokerage firms allow individuals from all walks of life to ride the wild roller coaster that is the stock market. Retail brokerages make money primarily through commissions on the trades of their clients, though brokerage firms are trying to move their customers to fee-based management. The retail brokerage industry includes not only full-service brokers such as Merrill Lynch and Morgan Stanley but also a number of discount and online brokers as well as the rarefied realm of private client services or private banking. In recent years, everyone has been trying to get a piece of the action, and lines between these groups have blurred—Merrill offers online trading, Fidelity Investments has a discount brokerage, and Charles Schwab offers retail asset management for high-net-worth individuals through its U.S. Trust subsidiary.

In addition to brokers, retail brokerage operations include trading desks, back-office operations to process transactions, compliance officers to ensure that traders and brokers don't engage in illegal activity, and research departments. Note, though, that most of the sell-side research at brokerage firms is in support of the capital markets units. In and of themselves research departments are often cost centers, a situation exacerbated by the conflict-of-interest scandal and Wall Street's settlement with corruption hound Eliot Spitzer. These days, research is pretty much barred from helping investment bankers reel in new clients.

Full-Service Brokerages

Full-service brokerages facilitate securities trading and act as financial advisors for individuals—recommending stocks, allocating asset portfolios, and executing orders. Many banks and financial services firms have acquired brokerage entities to become one-stop shops for all of an individual's financial needs—personal loans, mortgages, life insurance—in addition to traditional brokerage services. Citigroup, the nation's largest bank, added a full-service brokerage to its product offering when it merged with Travelers in 1998 and gained Wall Street titan Salomon Smith Barney. Merrill Lynch dominates the industry, with—first put your pinkie finger against the corner of mouth and purse your lips—$1.4 trillion in client assets and 14,100 financial advisors. Chasing Merrill are Citigroup's Smith Barney, then Wachovia Securities, and Morgan Stanley.

Discount and Online Brokerages

Charles Schwab pioneered the world of discount brokerages with his experiment in discount brokerages in 1974. Today, Schwab is the world's largest discount brokerage firm. Other firms have followed suit. E-Trade, Ameritrade, and Scottrade offer bare bones service (no advice, no hand holding) in exchange for low commissions and technology-rich websites. Today, however, the skies look pretty gray for discount brokerages. As firms such as Merrill Lynch offer fixed-price online trading, companies such as Fidelity expand into the low-end brokerage market, and assets of young investors trickle to a halt, the industry continues onward with consolidation and restructuring. Ameritrade purchased Datek in 2002 to shore up its position in a dwindling market. Schwab has moved away from its discount roots and has begun offering full-service features to wealthy investors through its acquisition of U.S. Trust. Meanwhile, the major firms have become engaged in a price war, slashing per-trade fees for what is essentially a commodities business: online stock trades.

Private Client Services

Private client services are the gravy train of top-tier brokerage houses. Even Goldman Sachs, best known for advising corporations on big mergers and IPOs, extends its Midas touch to wealthy individuals through its private client services operation. Private client services groups, like full-service retail brokerages, offer investors a full plate of investment vehicles to meet their individual needs. However, unlike ordinary investors, wealthy investors (usually accredited investors—people with a net worth of more than

$1,000,000 or household income of $200,000-plus) are able to invest in a wide range of unregulated securities and investment devices. The ante you need to pony up as an investor to get into private banking varies. Those catering to the "ultra high-net-worth" set keep the hoi polloi out with asset requirements of $25 million. Other firms court the McMansion set, requiring its clients to lay down a mere $500,000. Firms typically charge a management fee as a percentage of this service rather than a commission.

Unlike most retail brokerages, private banks regularly recruit newly minted MBAs. Top private bankers include UBS Private Banking, Goldman Sachs, Merrill Lynch, Morgan Stanley, Credit Suisse, J.P. Morgan Chase, Citigroup Private Bank, and Neuberger Berman.

INDEPENDENT RESEARCH COMPANIES

One man's tragedy is another man's opportunity. With the besmirching of the reputations of the investment bank–affiliated brokerage houses, independent equity research companies, whose opinions are uninfluenced by I-banking prerogatives, are getting a boost. Independent research firms fill their ranks with analysts who evaluate companies in a variety of industries as well as teams of bond analysts. As research analysis requires insight into the industry as much as it does an understanding of finance principles, companies often look for people with industry experience. Research companies typically split along the lines of client base; they cater either to the institutional or the individual investor, with far more firms specializing in institutional research. For the most part, firms sell their research on a subscription basis.

Sanford C. Bernstein, now a subsidiary of Alliance Capital Management, leads the pack of institutional investor–oriented research firms. Other companies servicing the segment include Sidoti & Co., Argus Research, Equity Research Associates, Vista Research, and CFRA (Center for Financial Research & Analysis). Firms serving individual investors include Value Line, Weiss Ratings, and Morningstar. Most independent researchers run on a pretty small scale. Even the largest firms such as Value Line and Sidoti only employ 70 and 50 analysts, respectively.

Industry Rankings

Top Asset Management Companies, as of March 31, 2005

Rank	Company	Assets Under Management ($M)	1-Year Change (%)
1	State Street Global Advisors	1,400,000	17
2	Barclays Global Investors[1]	1,360,000	18
3	Fidelity Investments	1,097,000	42
4	Vanguard Group[1]	800,000	10
5	J.P. Morgan Fleming Asset Management	791,000	42
6	Deutsche Asset Management[1]	730,500	3
7	Capital Group[1]	600,000	20
8	Northern Trust Global Investments[1]	572,000	11
9	Alliance Capital Management[2]	522,000	14
10	UBS Global Asset Management	531,000	15
11	Citigroup Asset Management[1]	514,000	−3
12	Prudential Financial	496,000	15
13	Merrill Lynch Investment Managers	458,000	−8
14	AIG Global Investment Group	493,000	25
15	Wellington Management Co.	470,000	13
16	Goldman Sachs Asset Management	463,000	23
17	PIMCO	445,000	19
18	Morgan Stanley Investment Management[1]	424,000	−18
19	Franklin Templeton Investments	412,000	23
20	MetLife[1]	387,000	11
21	TIAA-CREF	345,000	12
22	BlackRock	391,000	27
23	Credit Suisse Asset Management	335,000	35
24	Banc of America Capital Management[1]	229,000	−32
25	Putnam Investments[3]	194,000	−19

[1]As of December 31, 2004. [2]As of April 30, 2005. [3]As of May 2005.

Note: Fidelity, only mutual fund assets under management. Sources: Company reports; WetFeet analysis.

Top Retail Brokerage Companies

Firm	2004 Client Assets ($M)	1-Year Change (%)	Revenue ($M)	Employees
Merrill Lynch GPC	1,400,000	9	9,831	n/a
Smith Barney (Citigroup)	978,000	7	6,500	n/a
Charles Schwab	733,000	8	4,188	14,200
Wachovia Securities	652,500	13	4,400	19,000
Morgan Stanley	602,000	7	4,615	n/a
Fidelity Personal Investments	588,300	40	n/a	n/a
UBS Financial Services	533,968	4	4,256	17,388
Edward Jones	357,000	43	2,891	31,400
A.G. Edwards	312,000	26	2,608	15,390
TD Waterhouse Investor Services	172,300	–2	n/a	n/a
Bank of America Investment Services	149,000	67	n/a	4,000
Raymond James & Associates	136,000	36	1,829	n/a
E-Trade	88,100	24	924	3,320
Ameritrade	79,900	23	922	1,961
Piper Jaffray	51,000	2	355	3,027
American Express Financial Advisors	n/a	n/a	7,035	n/a

Notes: E-Trade revenue and assets for brokerage segment, staff for entire firm; Schwab figures exclude institutional business; Edward Jones data is from parent, The Jones Financial Companies; UBS revenue is operating income.
Sources: WetFeet analysis; Hoover's; SEC EDGAR Database.

Industry Trends

COMMISSIONS TO FEES

The retail brokerage industry is weaning itself from its traditional reliance on trade-based commissions by offering more and more fee-based services, which provide a more regular revenue stream in a volatile market. The fee structure also helps insulate firms from appearances of conflicts of interest as the fee is usually a percentage of assets under management, which means that it's in everyone's interest to see those assets grow. Firms usually charge investors 1.1 to 1.5 percent of assets, according to Cerulli Associates. Fees represent a growing slice of the industry's top-line income: At the beginning of the decade, fees accounted for less than 10 percent of revenues; by 2003, they accounted for 25 percent. One observer expects fees could account for over 70 percent of activity by decade-end. Moving toward a fee-based model can backfire if it's done without enough customer buy-in, however. In April 2005, the National Association of Securities Dealers (NASD) slapped Raymond James Financial with a fine totaling nearly $900,000 for allegedly transferring clients to fee-based accounts without determining whether that was the most appropriate structure for the clients.

SCANDAL DU JOUR: TIMING IS EVERYTHING

The financial services industry hit the Comstock Lode of scandals after the bubble burst, with regulators targeting nearly every corner of Wall Street for working against the best interests of their clients. By 2005, mutual fund firms and brokerages appeared to have put the worst of the probes behind them and were dealing with the fall-out. For brokers, that's meant a higher "Chinese Wall" between the investment bank and research departments, to eliminate the chance that an analyst might tout a company to the public in one breath—thereby pleasing company management who would hope-fully then push lucrative investment banking business their way—while disparaging the firm in private.

It wasn't just the Armani-pinstripe power broker whose dealings felt the sting of the regulatory whip this decade. The Dockers-wearing mutual fund manager also saw his industry's dirty laundry aired in public, causing massive asset withdrawals at some of the worst culprits. Putnam Investments, Strong Funds, Pilgrim Baxter, and Janus Capital were accused of short-trading in their own funds for certain executives' personal benefit or allowing preferred customers to trade fund shares after hours. The upshot for clients is that fund companies have restricted loosey-goosey trades in mutual funds and generally disclose more to shareholders about how they're spending money, particularly if these commissions could undermine the best price or choice for the investor. The upshot for the industry can be summed up in three words: settlements and suits. Financial services firms had paid $4.5 billion in fines by mid-2004, estimates *Forbes*. Meanwhile, the number of private securities lawsuits seeking class action status filed against U.S. companies rose 16 percent in 2004, according to PricewaterhouseCoopers.

INSIDER TIP

Brokers and asset managers of all shapes and sizes are looking for professionals that can court and advise well-heeled customers. Just make sure you know your claret from your Beaujolais.

THE BROKERAGE MODEL RETHUNK

During the trading frenzy of the late '90s, virtual brokers such as E-Trade and Ameritrade were the vehicles of choice for the savvy day trader. But with the market showing an obstinate refusal to go in directions other than north, online brokers have had trouble regaining steady and growing trading volume. Meanwhile, investors increasingly appear to be seeking experienced advice and are willing to pay reasonable incremental costs for help in navigating the current turbulent markets. Though the market rebounded in 2003 and late 2004, retail brokerages have focused on keeping a neat bottom line and resisted aggressive hiring. This is due in no small part to the costs associated with training new brokers—analysts estimate that a full-service brokerage pays about $250,000 to train a new broker and that even seasoned brokers cost firms $150,000 a year.

Some have responded to the changed marketplace by consolidating, others by reshuffling management. Wachovia and Prudential have formed a brokerage joint venture. Bank of America purchased FleetBoston and gained its discount brokerage subsidiary Quick & Reilly. Charles Schwab booted out its long-time CEO and brought back the discount broker's founder. Meanwhile, brokers led by Merrill Lynch have been waging a turf war with a body of investment advisors called financial planners, who are disputing the brokerage industry's move to asset-based investment advising.

FOLLOW THE MONEY

As small-time investors have shown less of a desire to move their rainy day funds into the stock market since the crash of 2000, brokerages and asset managers have hit on this strategy: go after the individuals whose nest eggs are so large that they'll look for investment strategies, regardless of what the market is doing. The increasing wealth of the Baby Boom generation has played a role in this thinking. Nearly every firm has some service targeted at the wealthy, with descriptions of what "wealthy" means ranging from $1 million to $100 million in assets. For more moderate-income customers, the trend has meant saying good-bye to some personalized brokerage service. Merrill Lynch and Morgan Stanley have reportedly tweaked their compensation structure so that brokers get paid less or not at all for handling trades on accounts that fall below a certain asset level, thus discouraging them from taking on smaller customers.

For job seekers, the wealth trend is worth noting because brokers and asset managers of all shapes and sizes are looking for professionals that can court and advise well-heeled customers. Just make sure you know your claret from your Beaujolais.

HEDGING IS THE BET

Once thought arcane, volatile, and the province of Nobel Prize winners such as Myron Scholes, hedge funds have suddenly become arcane, volatile, and wildly popular. Drawn by the potential to make millions, if not tens of millions, each year, MBAs are pounding on the doors of these firms.

Their track record in down markets—hedge funds consistently beat mutual funds when indexes fall—has piqued the interest of smaller investors, even as their records start to look slightly less stellar. The firms, in turn, have noticed. Some hedge funds accept investments as little as $25,000 from individual investors. Asset managers have launched funds of hedge funds—vehicles that use some of the same investing techniques as a traditional hedge fund, such as short-selling, but mitigate the risk by spreading the investment across several hedge funds. Institutional investors such as pension funds and foundations still account for a big part of hedge fund contributions. Regardless of who's investing, their numbers have grown so much that they now equal the number of mutual funds. Compared to about 100 in the early '90s, investors can now choose from about 8,000 hedge funds.

The Companies

Largest Asset Managers and Mutual Funds

Top Retail Brokerage Companies

Additional Asset Management Companies

Largest Asset Managers and Mutual Funds

The asset management companies profiled here are listed in alphabetical order. See the "Industry Rankings" section in the previous chapter for tables ranking firms by total assets under management.

ALLIANCE CAPITAL MANAGEMENT L.P.

1345 Avenue of the Americas
New York, NY 10105
Phone: 212-969-1000
Fax: 212-969-2229
www.alliancecapital.com

Nearly two-thirds owned by French insurance giant AXA and 30 percent by Alliance Capital Holdings, Alliance Capital is one of the largest investment management companies in the United States, with more than $539 billion of assets under management at year-end 2004. The acquisition of independent research firm Sanford C. Bernstein in 2000 rounded out Alliance Capital's offerings for private and high-net-worth clients, as well as complemented the firm's growth-style investing with value-focused products. Now, assets managed for institutions made up 58 percent of client assets, and assets in value-style stocks make up over 31 percent.

Headquartered in New York City, Alliance Capital has a presence in 36 cities worldwide. Its roster includes 4,100 employees and its institutional research arm employs more than 100 analysts. The firm suffered from the 2003 mutual fund scandal, which caused several company executives to resign and sent 2003 sales plunging by 40 percent. Its fortunes rebounded in 2004. Revenue at the publicly traded company rose 11 percent to $3 billion, and its share price gained nearly 29 percent.

AMERICAN INTERNATIONAL GROUP, INC.

70 Pine Street
New York, NY 10270
Phone: 212-770-7000
Fax: 212-509-9705
www.aig.com

When corruption-hound and New York State Attorney General Eliot Spitzer finished routing out wrongdoing in the mutual fund industry, he turned to the wide but unglamorous field of commercial insurance broking. And American International Group, the biggest insurer, was directly in his firing line. The subsequent investigation by the SEC and the state, which focused on whether the firm colluded with insurance brokers engaged in bid-rigging and whether AIG had artificially inflated results, led to big changes at the firm. Its stock plunged and long-time chief Hank Greenberg relinquished his leadership in March 2005.

Its bruised reputation hasn't lessened AIG's overall presence in asset management and brokerage. Its institutional arm, AIG Global Investment Management, manages $475.9 billion in assets, about half of which are fixed income. It employs 1,500 staff worldwide, including 450 investment professionals.

On the retail side, AIG has cobbled together a retirement savings division called AIG SunAmerica. Under that heading falls AIG Advisor Group, an umbrella for several independent broker-dealers such as Advantage Capital and FSC Securities. AIG Advisor Group is the third-largest independent-contractor broker-dealer by fee revenue and counts 5,000 financial advisors in its ranks. (Independent contractors are self-employed financial advisors who use the infrastructure and some of the offerings of broker-dealers like AIG.) AIG SunAmerica employs about 2,500 people and is based in Los Angeles. Annuities, as with most insurers, are a strong spot for the firm.

BANC OF AMERICA CAPITAL MANAGEMENT/ COLUMBIA MANAGEMENT GROUP

100 Federal Street
Boston, MA 02110
Phone: 617-434-2200
www.columbiamanagement.com

In keeping with its name, Bank of America has its sights set on the whole nation. While not quite there yet, the Charlotte, North Carolina–based descendent of NationsBank has been gobbling up regional banks on both coasts and is now the country's third-largest bank company by assets. A recent conquest, Northeast power-house FleetBoston, came with $160 billion-asset Columbia Management Group. The parent is now combining its existing asset management operation, Banc of America Capital Management, with Columbia and will keep the Columbia name.

The combined asset management group had $331 billion in assets under management at year-end 2004. Some 64 percent belong to institutions. Equity investments made up 38 percent of assets, while 47 percent were in money market funds and 15 percent in fixed income. Units within the group include mutual funds under the Columbia and Nations brands, equities, fixed income, quantitative strategies, and product marketing. Portfolio analysts generally work out of Boston, New York, Chicago, and Portland, Oregon.

BARCLAYS GLOBAL INVESTORS, N.A.

45 Fremont Street
San Francisco, CA 94105
Phone: 415-597-2000
Fax: 415-597-2271
www.barclaysglobal.com

Barclays Global Investors (BGI) made a name for itself in the '70s when it virtually invented index funds—funds whose holdings are selected by complicated computer models rather than amply paid managers, thus lowering their costs. Indexing remains one of its major strategies today, accounting for about two-thirds of its business. But it also manages $281 billion in active and enhanced index funds. Nearly 80 percent of BGI's 2,600 clients are either public entities or corporations, including corporate titans such as Citibank and Exxon Mobil.

With $1.36 trillion in assets under management, BGI consistently places among the largest asset management firms in the world. Some of its recent success in attracting client assets comes from the introduction of iShares, its ETFs that allow investors to buy and sell shares in what amounts to a tracking stock for various groups, from Chinese Internet companies to U.S. biotech firms. In 5 years, iShares have grown to account for half of all assets invested in the U.S. ETF market.

Headquartered in San Francisco, BGI's investment researchers also have outposts in London, Tokyo, and Sydney. It also has recently opened client-services offices from Singapore to Amsterdam. Overall, the company—a subsidiary's of Britain's Barclays PLC—employs approximately 2,000 people. The research arm, called the Advanced Strategies and Research Group in Barclay lingo, is responsible for creating the entire firm's managed portfolios. Ambitious BA, MBA, or PhD degree candidates might consider applying to a 1- to 2-year "development programme" that starts the summer before one's final year of study.

BLACKROCK, INC.

40 East 52nd Street
New York, NY 10022
Phone: 212-810-5300
Fax: 212-935-1370
www.blackrock.com

Founded in 1998, BlackRock has expanded from a boutique advisory firm known for its bond products to a more diversified asset manager and risk advisor with 1,000 employees and $342 billion in assets under management. In January 2005, it bought MetLife's State Street Research and Management and State Street Realty, boosting its equity, alternative investments, and hedge fund capabilities. It went public in 1999, though there's not much public float. Staff and the public own 29 percent, and PNC Financial owns 71 percent.

BlackRock prides itself on being a technological innovator, using software to analyze securities, assess portfolio risk, and move information. Its success in portfolio analytics, where many of its portfolio managers start, has been such that it's started to sell the analysis to other financial institutions. Employees usually work in one of five areas: asset management, which includes its private client and pension plan teams, portfolio management, global operations, portfolio administration, and BlackRock Solutions.

Besides its New York headquarters, the firm has offices in Boston; Edinburgh; Hong Kong; Morristown, New Jersey; San Francisco; Singapore; Sydney; Tokyo; and Wilmington, Delaware. BlackRock recruits mostly from Ivy League universities, big state schools in the Northeast and Southeast, and historically black colleges. But it does encourage candidates from outside farm schools to e-mail their resumes to careers@blackrock.com.

THE CAPITAL GROUP COMPANIES, INC.

333 South Hope Street
Los Angeles, CA 90071
Phone: 213-486-9200
Fax: 213-486-9217
www.capgroup.com

What, you haven't heard of The Capital Group? You're not alone. Founded in the dark year 1931, The Capital Group has quietly created the third-largest family of mutual funds in the country—better known as The American Funds. The company encompasses two divisions: Capital Research and Management, the investment advisor to American Funds, and Capital Guardian Trust and Capital International companies, which together provide global investment management services for individuals, corporate retirement plans, and institutional investors. Capital Research's assets under management top $600 billion, while assets managed by Capital Guardian Trust Company and the Capital International companies total about $300 billion. Together, they employ 6,000 people in 20 offices worldwide.

The company's lack of publicity says something about its culture as well; The Capital Group is known in the industry for its laid-back attitude and low ego quotient as well as a conservative investment style. Indeed, the company still promotes the values of its founder, Jonathan Bell Lovelace: research-driven investment, long-term focus, and integrity. The company has a very low attrition rate, tends to promote from within, and offers a generous benefits package common to the investment management industry.

CITIGROUP ASSET MANAGEMENT

399 Park Avenue, 7th Floor
New York, NY 10043
Phone: 212-559-1400
Fax: 212-793-3946
www.citigroupam.com

Citigroup Asset Management's history stretches back to the horse and buggy days of 1873, when Charles D. Barney opened the brokerage that would be later become known as Smith Barney. Today, the firm is an amalgamation of various well-known Wall Street investment houses, including Smith Barney, Salomon Brothers, and Shearson Lehman—all under the red umbrella of Citigroup, the biggest American bank.

CAM employs 395 investment professionals and manages $514 billion in assets from 16 investment and global research centers. Products include the Smith Barney family of more than 60 mutual funds and Salomon Brothers Asset Management's institutional offerings. Its parent and sister investment bank unit got dragged down into the conflict-of-interest scandals that followed the bursting of the dot-com bubble. But on the mutual fund side, CAM appeared to avoid the regulatory pogroms that plagued the industry in 2003. Nonetheless, the SEC did initiate an investigation into a Citigroup decision to use an outside servicer to serve as an internal-transfer agent for its mutual funds—allegedly only after the servicing firm directed its investment banking business to Citigroup affiliates.

CAM is part of the Citigroup Global Investment Management group, itself one of four business groups within the giant Citigroup organization. Would-be Citibankers should note that the Citigroup Private Bank, while technically not part of CAM, offers a 3-year program for MBAs and undergrads.

CREDIT SUISSE ASSET MANAGEMENT LIMITED

U.S. Headquarters:
466 Lexington Avenue
New York, NY 10017
Phone: 212-875-3500
Fax: 646-658-0728
www.csam.com

A subsidiary of Swiss-American investment bank Credit Suisse First Boston, Credit Suisse Asset Management (CSAM) handles $342 billion in client assets, some 34 percent of which are fixed income. The company came into being in 1997 when Credit Suisse consolidated its 17 boutique asset management companies. In 1999, CSAM acquired Warburg Pincus and folded in Donaldson, Lufkin & Jenrette's asset management arm a year later. The company's platter of investments for institutional and wealthy investors include hedge funds, private equity, derivative investments, along with the staple equity and fixed-income products.

CSAM employs 1,885 worldwide and as of mid-2003, counted 312 portfolio managers in its ranks. They work out of 12 global locations but mostly from its five core investment centers of London, New York, Zurich, Sydney, and Tokyo. In the United States, CSAM employs 410 and manages $27 billion in assets. CSAM touts its flat management structure (only four promotions before making managing director!) and says it recruits from a wide range of academic backgrounds, since "training on the job is the most effective way to learn, understand, and drive our business."

DEUTSCHE ASSET MANAGEMENT

U.S. Headquarters:
60 Wall Street, 21st floor
New York, NY 10005
Phone: 212-250-2500
www.deam.com

Deutsche Bank's asset management arm, part of the company's Private Client and Asset Management group, offers both retail and institutional products in the United States and throughout the world. DeAM, as company insiders refer to it, employs 8,000 people in major financial centers worldwide and manages $731 billion in assets for clients in more than 60 countries. In Europe, its retail DWS Investments unit controls about 25 percent of the German mutual fund market. In the United States, DeAM fleshed out its financial advisor capabilities when it bought Scudder Investments in 2002 for $2.5 billion.

Deutsche had a leg-up on the competition when the real estate market boomed over the past few years. DB Real Estate employs 700 real estate professionals in 16 offices worldwide; they manage high-yielding, proprietary real estate investments and investments in publicly traded real estate investment trusts, or REITs.

Parent Deutsche Bank invites undergrad, master's, and PhD candidates to apply to one of its summer and full-time analyst or associate programs.

FMR CORP. (FIDELITY INVESTMENTS)

82 Devonshire Street
Boston, MA 02109
Phone: 617-563-7000
Fax: 617-476-6150
www.fidelity.com

The largest mutual fund manager, if you count money-market mutual funds, and the country's top 401(k) provider, Fidelity has nearly $960 billion in mutual fund assets under management and runs 360 mutual funds. Once best known for its flagship Magellan Fund, managed by name-brand fund manager Peter Lynch, Fidelity has since spread out to retail brokerage, IRAs, 401(k)s, life insurance, and even start-up financing. Like other big fund companies, Fidelity—or Fido, as it's sometimes called in the industry—has been slashing expenses on its index funds in a bid to lure more investors.

In early 2005, Fido announced it would spin-off its institutional arm into a separate firm. It's first investing $100 million in the project and hiring 100 investment professionals to bulk up the unit, which will manage $102 billion in corporate and public pension assets. Although Fidelity entered 2005 untainted by the fund-trading scandal, regulators have opened an inquiry into whether Fidelity traders awarded stock business to certain brokers who had given them excessive gifts.

The company is privately held, with the founding Johnson family owning about half. Johnson family scion Abigail Johnson owns nearly 30 percent of the company herself and recently switched positions from president of the mutual fund division to president of the retirement division. Its private structure means that Fidelity can spend $700 million on upgrading its online brokerage without worrying about the next quarterly earnings report.

Fidelity increased its staff 13 percent in 2004 to more than 32,000 employees. Because the company has a policy of hiring fund managers from within, it views the selection of analysts as critical to the success of the company. Early on, company interviewers plumb applicants' personal interests to find a fit (e.g., a person with a bent for baseball statistics might transfer that interest into evaluating companies). Once in action, analysts have a lot of flexibility in how they choose to pick stocks; the firm believes there's no one perfect investment style.

FRANKLIN TEMPLETON INVESTMENTS

1 Franklin Parkway
Building 970, 1st Floor
San Mateo, CA 94403
Phone: 800-632-2350 or 650-312-2000
Fax: 650-312-5606
www.franklintempleton.com

Franklin Resources, the parent company of Franklin Templeton mutual funds, settled a number of state and regulatory investigations in 2004, and in August of that year agreed to a $50 million settlement over mutual timing charges. Despite the bad publicity, Franklin—which trades under the clever ticker BEN—managed to increase assets under management by 20 percent to $402.2 billion. Its staff ranks gained 5 percent to 6,779 working in 28 countries.

The company's mutual funds run the gamut of traditional investments, from domestic to international, taxable to tax-free, stocks to bonds. The company has been expanding its grasp steadily. In 2000, Franklin bought out a joint venture partner in South Korea, becoming the first fully foreign-owned investment trust management company in the country. The founding Johnson family still own a big chunk of available shares and holds senior positions: half-brothers Charles and Rupert hold the titles of chairman and vice chairman, respectively, while Charles' son Gregory is co-CEO.

The company offers several ways in if you're working toward your undergraduate or MBA degree. Its 2-year research associate program aims to mold its charges into a bona fide stock or bond picker. And remember, it's one of the few big asset management firms where you can enjoy the sunny West Coast lifestyle while making Wall Street bucks.

GOLDMAN SACHS ASSET MANAGEMENT

85 Broad Street
New York, NY 10004
Phone: 212-902-1000
Fax: 212-902-3000
www.gs.com

Goldman Sachs tries to be the gold standard in its main businesses, which include investment banking, trading and principal investments, and investment management. While not as prominent as its investment banking sibling, Goldman Sachs's investment group has built a 24-karat business around U.S.-based and global mutual funds, managed accounts, nontraditional investments and hedge funds, and private equity placements. At the end of February 2005, it had $482 billion in assets under management, 17 percent higher than the year earlier. Investment management includes private wealth management, which advises affluent individuals, and Goldman Sachs Asset Management, which administers to pension funds, endowments, and other institutions.

Goldman offers a similar program for its asset management recruits as it does for its investment bankers. Undergrads can apply to a 2-year financial analyst position in its investment management group. MBA and other advanced-degree holders who have already spent 2 to 5 years in the workforce can apply to an associate program. Within the asset management group, jobs include equity research, quantitative resources, bond and currency analysis, and client relationship management. Goldman has offices in 24 countries and employs nearly 21,000 people.

J.P. MORGAN ASSET MANAGEMENT

522 Fifth Avenue
New York, NY 10036
Phone: 212-483-2323
www.jpmorgan.com/assetmanagement

J.P. Morgan Asset Management (the firm was known as J.P. Morgan Fleming Asset Management until very recently), the investment arm of J.P. Morgan Chase, is a giant begotten of successive mergers. In 2000, Chase Manhattan Bank bought prestigious British investment firm Robert Fleming Holdings. Then Chase merged with J.P. Morgan. Another big mega-merger, this time the 2004 link-up with Chicago-based Bank One, brought One's retail asset management into the J.P. Morgan fold.

J.P. Morgan Asset Management now has $791 billion in assets under management, two million retail clients and operates the fifth-largest mutual fund complex in the United States. Its parent also owns discount broker BrownCo.

Candidates with an undergraduate degree and GPA of 3.2 and higher can apply to the 3-year analyst program at J.P. Morgan Funds, which manages 101 funds. As a new analyst, one is first immersed in a 5-week training program taught by senior Morgan managers and professors. Duties as an analyst include product analysis, stock research, and developing sales and marketing programs.

MERRILL LYNCH INVESTMENT MANAGERS

800 Scudders Mill Road
Plainsboro, NJ 08536
Phone: 609-282-1212
www.mlim.ml.com

Merrill Lynch Investment Managers (MLIM) is the asset management arm of Merrill Lynch, managing $496 billion in client assets at the end of 2004. Its staff works closely with Merrill's retail brokerage arm, the Global Private Client Group. MLIM's equity and fixed-income mutual funds and asset management services are tailored to retail, high-net-worth, and institutional investors. Retail and institutional assets make up 92 percent of total assets. The unit offers over 100 of its own mutual funds through the Private Client Group's 14,000 financial advisors and other channels.

MLIM employs 2,500 people in 17 countries and gained more employees than it lost in 2004. It doesn't have a recruitment program for MBAs. But for those with under-graduate degrees, MLIM recruits for analyst positions that cut across all parts of the organization, including investments, marketing, sales, and operations. The typical route is securing a summer internship right before your senior year; if all goes well, you'll return to campus with a full-time offer in hand. Unlike typical investment banking analyst positions, MLIM doesn't grind down its new recruits for 2 years and then boot them out to other Wall Street firms or MBA programs. Instead, MLIM sees the analyst position as the first step in what it hopes will be a long career at the firm. It'll reimburse employees for class tuition and fees incurred from reaching that gold standard of the asset management industry, the CFA. "We want to make sure we're looking at internal mobility, so they can grow in their career and make the next step here, not somewhere else," said one insider.

MLIM mostly recruits from East Coast schools. Analysts largely work from its corporate Princeton campus.

MORGAN STANLEY INVESTMENT MANAGEMENT

1221 Avenue of the Americas
New York, NY 10020
Phone: 212-762-7100 or 800-422-6464
www.morganstanley.com/im

Morgan Stanley Investment Management handles $424 billion in client assets for a range of institutional clients, including companies, endowments, and unions. It also has a special team to service consultants who advise institutional retirement plans on investments. Sister unit Morgan Stanley Private Wealth Management caters to individuals, families, and foundations with more than $10 million in investing assets out of 16 offices in the United States and abroad.

Morgan Stanley Investment Management is the asset management arm of blue-chip investment bank and brokerage Morgan Stanley. The parent spent the spring of 2005 embroiled in a management struggle between CEO Philip Purcell, who hailed from the decidedly non-blue-chip Dean Witter brokerage, and former Wall Street deal makers who owned shares in the company and were dissatisfied with Purcell's performance.

Morgan Stanley offers analyst and associate positions in investment management. Both generally start in the global investor group, sales and marketing, or operations. Analysts with recent BA's or BS's may be located in New York City; West Conshohocken, Pennsylvania; Oakbrook, Illinois; Houston; and Jersey City. The Private Wealth Management Group recruits MBAs for a 5-month associate program that begins in New York City.

NORTHERN TRUST CORPORATION

50 South LaSalle Street
Chicago, IL 60675
Phone: 312-630-6000
Fax: 312-630-1512
www.northerntrust.com

Founded in 1889, Northern Trust is one of the old-line wealth managers and spent much of the last century managing the fortunes of rich Midwesterners. It still advises 20 percent of the nation's richest families, including members of the Bush dynasty, according to one report. But Northern Trust has increasingly set its sight overseas. In March 2005 it bought the financial services arm of London's Baring Asset Management. It has offices in Singapore, Luxembourg, the United Kingdom, and four other foreign countries, and plans to open more. As of December 2004, Northern Trust counted $572 billion in assets under management, $2.6 trillion in assets under administration, and $44 billion in bank assets.

The firm consists of two business units: Personal Financial Services and Corporate and Institutional Services. Personal Financial Services offers trust administration, private banking, residential real estate mortgage lending, and brokerage and investment management services to small businesses and individuals. Corporate and Institutional Services provides trust, global custody, investment retirement, commercial banking, and treasury management services worldwide.

In the United States, the company offers two 15- to 24-month, entry-level tracks. The "Gold Program" can lead to careers in investments, relationship management, credit services, and operations. The portfolio accounting analyst track preps new recruits for jobs in investment accounting and consulting.

PACIFIC INVESTMENT MANAGEMENT COMPANY, LLC (PIMCO)

840 Newport Center Drive, Suite 300
Newport Beach, CA 92660
Phone: 949-720-6000 or 800-746-2602
Fax: 949-720-1376
www.pimco.com

The gentlemen of PIMCO prefer bonds. Away from the hustle and bustle of Wall Street, PIMCO is one of the largest specialists in fixed-income products and has a reputation for knowing what's up when yields drop. Chief Investment Officer Bill Gross frequently appears on all-business cable shows when the Federal Reserve is about to make a rate move. This Southern California company's preference for bonds has served it well as the equity markets roiled investors. While other money managers lost assets, PIMCO's shot up by more than 25 percent in 2002 and nearly 30 percent in 2003. Growth has slowed somewhat as the equity markets moved into bull territory. Nonetheless, assets under management climbed 19 percent in 2004 to $445 billion. The company credits its success to a total return approach and long-term focus. Innovation has helped as well. In order to allay concerns that rising inflation would cut into bond fund returns, PIMCO has rolled out a series of inflation-protected funds.

Like California's leading politician, PIMCO has strong Teutonic links; it is a subsidiary of Germany's insurance giant Allianz. Although it doesn't have the extensive analyst associate programs of some fund firms, PIMCO does offer a wide range of flexibility for people who know what they want as well as a flat organization that grants responsibility early on. PIMCO offers opportunities in its portfolio management, account management, and business management divisions. Besides its home base of Newport Beach, PIMCO has offices in New York, London, Tokyo, Singapore, Sydney, and Munich.

PRUDENTIAL FINANCIAL, INC.

751 Broad Street
Newark, NJ 07102
Phone: 973-802-6000 or 800-346-3778
Fax: 973-802-4479
www.prudential.com

Along with Springsteen, Sinatra, and Bon Jovi, New Jersey can count Prudential Financial among its assets. An affiliate of Prudential Insurance Company of America, the investment management division has boosted its business with a steady diet of acquisitions. Pru followed the 2003 acquisition of annuities distributor American Skandia with two deals in 2004—one for a South Korean asset management firm owned by Hyundai Investment & Securities, the other for Cigna's retirement business. At the end of 2004, it managed roughly $500 billion in assets.

The firm offers a wide range of institutional and individual asset management products, from the standard mutual fund management to commercial mortgage securitizations. In 2003 it formed a brokerage joint venture with Wachovia Securities in which Prudential has a 38 percent stake. And it offers three money management programs to guide individual investors through the fund-picking process. The company didn't come through the scandal-ridden first part of the decade completely unscathed. In 2004 it agreed to pay the NASD a $2 million fine to settle accusations of annuity fraud.

It's diversity efforts have won kudos: For 4 straight years, the National Association for Female Executives has named it one of the top-10 companies for executive women.

PUTNAM LLC

1 Post Office Square
Boston, MA 02109
Phone: 617-292-1000 or 800-225-1581
Fax: 617-482-3610
www.putnam.com

This old-school Boston mutual fund company has seen its reputation grow more tarnished than Paul Revere's original pewter mug, as a series of regulatory scandals have cast the firm and its parent in a less-than-responsible light. In 2003, the company became the first charged in the industry's mutual fund trading scandal and endured stories and accusations of certain shareholders skirting company policy to late-trade in fund shares.

Then, just as it was recovering from these allegations, New York State's attorney general levied charges of insurance bid-rigging against Putnam parent Marsh & McLennan.

Putnam has done its best to put the phrase "regulatory probe" behind it. It's made a $110 million settlement with the SEC and Massachusetts regulators, adopted reforms based on new mutual fund protection principles, replaced its CEO, and lowered the costs of owning a mutual fund. Nevertheless, assets under management fell 11 percent to $213 billion in 2004, and its head count has shrunk to 3,700. Its client roster is still impressive, however: Putnam serves 264 institutional clients and 10 million shareholders and retirement plan participants. The firm employs 230 investment professionals in offices in Boston, London, and Tokyo.

STATE STREET GLOBAL ADVISORS

1 Lincoln Street
Boston, MA 02111
Phone: 617-786-3000
Fax: 617-664-4299
www.statestreet.com

The sleeping giant of the asset management world, State Street Corp. quietly manages the most pension funds in the United States, while its trust and custody departments make it the top servicer of U.S. mutual and pension fund assets. Oh yeah, and its $1.4 trillion in assets under management make it the largest by that measure as well. State Street Global Advisors, its asset management arm, is primarily an institutional asset manager, investing in passive equity funds, active quantitative and fundamental equity funds, fixed-income, real estate, currency, and absolute return vehicles. The parent company, among other important roles, calculates most of the mutual fund prices that appear every day in the paper.

Although headquartered in Boston, State Street has offices in 25 countries and employs more than 19,000 people. The firm runs a network of 28 offices and employs 405 investment professionals. It's proud of being the first to launch an ETF with the Standard & Poor's Depository Receipts in 1993. The firm recruits for investment support roles such as fund accountants, portfolio administrators, and tax claim coordinators.

TIAA-CREF

730 3rd Avenue
New York, NY 10017
Phone: 212-490-9000 or 800-842-2252
Fax: 212-916-4840
www.tiaa-cref.com

TIAA-CREF (the Teachers Insurance and Annuity Association–College Retirement Equities Fund) is one of the largest private pension managers around, keeping nest eggs warm for 3.2 million academics at 15,000 institutions. The company started in 1918 when the Teachers Insurance and Annuity Association was created with a $1 million endowment from the Carnegie Foundation. In 1952, the company created an annuity fund for investors, the College Retirement Equities Fund. The nonprofit offers savings products to the general public, but its typical customer tends to be in the academic, research, medical, or cultural sector. TIAA-CREFF recently opened 16 new offices in college towns such as Cambridge, Massachusetts, and Palo Alto, California.

The company's 5,700 employees help manage $345 billion in assets. TIAA-CREF is also the largest institutional real estate investor in the United States, with a $50 billion portfolio. TIAA-CREF has a reputation for being a progressive employer: *Fortune* has named it one of the 50 "Best Companies for Minorities."

UBS GLOBAL ASSET MANAGEMENT

51 West 52nd Street
New York, NY 10019
Phone: 212-882-5000
Fax: 212-882-5383
www.ubs.com/e/globalam.html

UBS Global Asset Management was formed by the 1998 Swiss mega-merger of UBS and Swiss Bank Corp. Today, the firm is the second-largest mutual fund manager in Europe and the largest fund manager in Switzerland. It has offices in 21 countries, with main offices in London, Chicago, New York, Tokyo, and Zurich.

UBS Global Asset Management has a staff of more than 2,600, 630 of whom are investment professionals. A large number of clients in the United States have helped boost assets under management to $527 billion, in no small part due to UBS's $11.8 billion acquisition of Paine Webber in 2000 (thank you, Paine Webber). The company offers products of both traditional equity and fixed-income investments, as well as alternative investments that include real estate and quantitative and hedge funds.

THE VANGUARD GROUP, INC.

100 Vanguard Boulevard
Malvern, PA 19355
Phone: 610-648-6000 or 800-662-7447
Fax: 610-669-6605
www.vanguard.com

Individual investor advocate John Bogle started Vanguard in 1975 in an effort to create low-cost funds. In keeping with the nautical theme of the company (the Vanguard was Admiral Horatio Nelson's first ship), Vanguard terms its 10,000 employees its "crew," the corporate cafeterias its "galleys," and so on. John Bogle's investment strategy has maintained Vanguard as a leader in low-management-fee funds. The company specializes in index funds (it claims to have created the first indexed mutual fund in 1976) and has grown to be the second-largest mutual fund company in the country as investors bet against their portfolio managers' ability to consistently beat the market. Like rival Fidelity, it's chipped away at the expense ratio on its largest indexes as one more way to pull in client assets.

Vanguard increased its assets under management by 10 percent in 2004 to more than $800 billion. In addition to ranking high in managed assets, Vanguard consistently gets accolades as an employer. *Essence* magazine ranked Vanguard as a top employer in 2004, as did *InformationWeek*, and the AARP. The company prides itself on efforts to create an equal opportunity workplace, including diversity training for managers and diversity "councils" that focus on ways to make the workplace more equitable. Vanguard recruits at colleges in Pennsylvania, among others.

WELLINGTON MANAGEMENT COMPANY, LLP

75 State Street
Boston, MA 02109
Phone: 617-951-5000
Fax: 617-951-5250
www.wellington.com

Though you've probably never heard of the company, Wellington Management has been investing other people's money since 1928. The company has the distinction of offering the first balanced mutual fund, the Wellington Fund. The Boston Brahmin has had a track record of slow but steady growth. It opened offices in San Francisco, Sydney, and Tokyo in 1997 and didn't open another until hanging out a shingle in Hong Kong in 2003. Worldwide, it has more than 1,000 clients. Along with its Boston headquarters, the firm has offices in Atlanta, Chicago, and Radnor, Pennsylvania.

The Boston-based private partnership is an institutional asset manager, advising institutional clients and mutual fund sponsors in more than 40 countries. By March 2005, it was managing $470 billion in assets, some 66 percent of which were in equities. The company is known for its morning meeting, in which the investment management team, including senior executives, gather to trade investment ideas.

The firm makes no bones about selecting future employees with the same care it takes in picking stocks. Many of its advertised positions seek experienced financial professionals, and its portfolio managers have an average 17 years of experience. More bluntly, it tells job seekers, "We're not right for everyone."

Top Retail Brokerage Companies

The profiles of the leading brokerages here appear in alphabetical order. This section includes retail brokerage as well as private banking operations. See the "Industry Rankings" section in the previous chapter to see rankings by total client assets.

A.G. EDWARDS, INC.

1 North Jefferson Avenue
St. Louis, MO 63103
Phone: 314-955-3000 or 877-835-7877
Fax: 314-955-5547
www.agedwards.com

Considered a Main Street, rather than Wall Street, broker, A.G. Edwards plays off its Midwestern roots. Founded in 1887, it is one of the country's oldest full-service brokerage firms. It matches every client with one of its nearly 7,000 financial advisors, who offer clients stocks, bonds, mutual funds, commodities, insurance, and mortgage products in a quota-free environment. Additionally, the company invests in private equity partnerships.

Like many other companies in the industry, A.G. Edwards has been keeping its staffing roster lean in recent years. It employs 15,390 people, which is 510 fewer than at the beginning of 2004 and well off its bull-market levels. Among them, some 50 senior analysts cover 700 companies in more than 70 industries. *Fortune* named it one of the "Best Companies to Work For" in 2005 for the tenth time. A.G. Edwards recruits recent graduates who have a bachelor's in finance and MBAs for investment analysis and investment banking positions.

AMERICAN EXPRESS FINANCIAL ADVISORS

50606 AXP Financial Center, H27/52
Minneapolis, MN 55474
Phone: 612-671-2711 or 800-386-2042
finance.americanexpress.com

American Express Financial Advisors (AEFA) is one three business segments of card and travel giant American Express Financial Corp.—but not for long. In February 2005, AmEx announced plans to spin off the division, which now describes its target clients as the "mass affluent." AEFA provides financial planning, brokerage services, insurance, and other investments through a network of 12,000 financial advisors in 700 offices, as well as the Internet and other channels.

In 2004 it made $7 billion in net revenue, up 15 percent from 2003 as its acquisition of U.K.-based Threadneedle Asset Management Holdings offset outflows from its AXP retail mutual funds. Like many others in the industry, American Express shelled out its share of regulatory fines, in its case a mere $13 million for alleged violations in selling mutual funds.

AMERITRADE HOLDING CORPORATION

4211 South 102nd Street

Omaha, NE 68127

Phone: 402-331-7856 or 800-237-8692

Fax: 402-597-7789

www.ameritradeholding.com

Pioneering online broker Ameritrade has been fighting tooth-and-nail to hang onto client assets even when the stock market goes sideways. After the individual investing bonanza of the late 1990s shut down, Ameritrade made several acquisitions that picked up additional customers and assets. Among them: Datek in 2002, assets of mydiscount-broker.com in 2003, and those of Bidwell & Co. in 2004. With trading activity still fragile, Ameritrade has been slashing fees for stock trades—as have its main rivals. In 2004, client assets rose 23 percent to $80 billion while revenue rose 26 percent.

Best known for giving mom-and-pop traders a cheap way to play Wall Street, Omaha-based Ameritrade also has an institutional client division. It continually launches new technical services and products designed to help traders manage their investments, and hopefully make more. Despite pressures facing all the online brokers, its service has won awards, including a 4-star rating in *Barron's* 2005 review of online brokers and the "Best Financial Services Customer Service" from J.D. Powers & Associates.

BANC OF AMERICA INVESTMENT SERVICES, INC.

Gateway Village 900 Building
900 West Trade Street
Charlotte, NC 28255
Phone: 1-800-926-1111
www.baisidirect.com

When Bank of America sealed its deal for FleetBoston in 2004, it inherited discount broker Quick & Reilly. Now the third-largest bank-owned brokerage and one of the biggest overall, BAI (as insiders call it) has more than 1.2 million accounts and $141 billion in total clients assets as of March 31, 2005. It provides online self-directed investing, with options for more active traders, plus investing via a personal financial advisor. BAI has more than 200 locations in 34 states.

THE CHARLES SCHWAB CORPORATION

101 Montgomery Street
San Francisco, CA 94104
Phone: 415-627-7000 or 800-435-4000
Fax: 415-636-5970
www.schwab.com

Schwab revolutionized the brokerage industry in 1974 with its discount brokerage service, and it continued to add innovation through the dot-com era, becoming one of the first brick-and-mortar companies to offer online trading. When the crash came, however, Schwab was hit hard, and it had to make several rounds of layoffs to bring operating expenses more in line with revenue. Schwab has moved up and along the food chain by offering "Signature" and private client services to high-net-worth customers, as it tries to replace trading commissions lost when day traders returned to their day jobs. It bought wealth manager U.S. Trust and also owns CyberTrader, a tech-rich online broker that targets serious, active traders.

Attempts to diversify its revenue beyond its retail core proved mostly unsuccessful. In 2004, less than a year after buying investment bank boutique Soundview Technology Group, Schwab sold its institutional units. That venture, combined with lackluster revenue, prompted Schwab's board to boot CEO David Pottruck and bring back founder Charles Schwab. The firm, with some difficulty, has tried to carve out a spot between the no-frills discount brokers and the full-service firms. It's opened investor branches and has rolled out an in-house equity selection service, even as it continues to cut rates on trades. In 2003, it launched a bank.

For a firm founded on the idea of letting investors choose their own investments, Schwab has done pretty well in the advice department. Its Equity Model Portfolio, which is based on its in-house stock-picking service, was ranked number one by

Barron's for the 2002–04 period, for the second time in a row. Contrary to its late '90s image as a mostly Web broker, it hires quite a few warm bodies to reach out to clients: It recruits financial consultants, its term for licensed brokers, with a proven track record. Compensation is based on revenue produced from the client's assets under management, and making $300,000 or more annually is not unheard of.

E-TRADE SECURITIES LLC

134 East 57th Street
New York, NY 10022
Phone: 646-521-4300 or 800-387-2331
Fax: 888-276-9771
www.etrade.com

E-Trade Financial Corp., whose ticker symbol is the whimsical ET, has fought hard to keep afloat in the postbubble stock market. It's tried to offset slowdowns in trading activity by pushing other financial products that the home investor might need. As a result, assets at its banking unit have climbed to $12 billion, and in 2004 net banking revenue made up 40 percent of total revenue. The firm bought online broker Tradescape in 2002. In 2005, it rolled out E-Trade Complete, an account that combines a customer's trading, investing, cash, and debt accounts. In May 2005, it launched a hostile takeover bid for rival Ameritrade. It hasn't been easy clinging to client assets when the stock market treads water, as it did in parts of 2004 and into 2005. The number of employees slipped in 2004 by 4 percent to 3,320. But revenue squeaked out a 6 percent gain that year.

Like many start-ups that survived the tech crash of 2000, E-Trade has shed much of its freewheeling dot-com identity. It moved its headquarters to New York City from Silicon Valley, and the corporate culture is more suit than sandals these days. E-Trade has also been busy expanding overseas and now has online sites in nine countries outside the United States. It came close to merging with rival TD Waterhouse in 2004. The firm recruits from California and some East Coast universities.

FIDELITY PERSONAL INVESTMENTS

82 Devonshire Street
Boston, MA 02109
Phone: 617-563-7000
Fax: 617-476-6150
personal.fidelity.com

Already a pioneer in the mutual fund industry, Fidelity hooked its wagon to the discount brokerage star and has become the sixth-largest retail brokerage in the country with $588 billion in customer assets and 9.9 million retail accounts. Customers access Fidelity through the company's award-winning website, through its call centers, or by visiting its financial centers. Fidelity advisors offer not only Fidelity funds and its 401(k) rollover plans, but also popular funds of other firms, stocks, fixed-income investments, and asset management services.

Its online brokerage, with little fanfare, has built a retail fortress of 5.9 million customer accounts with $429.5 billion assets held in online accounts. Fidelity Investments also operates 101 investor centers in 43 markets.

THE JONES FINANCIAL COMPANIES, L.L.L.P./ EDWARD JONES

12555 Manchester Road
Des Peres, MO 63131
Phone: 314-515-2000
Fax: 314-515-2622
www.edwardjones.com

Your stock brokerage is named Edward, you're headquartered in Missouri—that narrows it down to two. Hardly a second fiddle to A.G. Edwards, the brokerage subsidiary of The Jones Financial Companies has carved out a special brokerage niche. Its new brokers build their business the old-fashioned way—walking door-to-door and sweet-talking local store owners and housewives. And it's eschewed such newfangled brokerage contraptions as Internet trading.

Despite its iconoclast ways, Edward Jones has made strides where it counts. It received the highest customer satisfaction rating among 20 full-service brokerages ranked by J.D. Power & Associates. Its 5,800 associates own the firm in a partnership, a growing rarity among the big brokerages; this arrangement allows the firm to offer its brokers a liberal profit-sharing plan. Its squeaky-clean reputation was sullied in late 2004 when regulators accused Edward Jones brokers of guiding their customers to fund companies that, unbeknownst to the customer, were also paying the brokerage through an innocuous-sounding arrangement called "revenue sharing."

Note, undergrads, Jones is also one of the few full-service brokerages that accepts greenhorns fresh out of college for its broker training program. This, of course, encourages promotion from within. New brokers have defined goals that they must execute upon. They must make 25 real contacts a day and contact prospects at least once every 2 weeks before reaping the benefits of their own office with the name of Edward Jones (and the broker's) on the door. That process usually takes 8 to 11 months.

MERRILL LYNCH GLOBAL PRIVATE CLIENT GROUP

4 World Financial Center
250 Vesey Street
New York, NY 10080
Phone: 212-449-1000 or 800-637-7455
Fax: 212-449-7357
www.ml.com

Merrill Lynch is at or near the top in investment banking, institutional trading, and asset management. But perhaps most impressive is its retail brokerage operation. Clients keep $1.4 trillion in assets at Merrill Lynch Global Private Client Group, far more than at number-two broker Smith Barney. Global Private Client counts 14,100 financial advisors in its ranks, who work out of 600 offices around the world. "This is the bread and butter of Merrill," says one insider.

Indeed, the unit leaves few slices in the investing loaf untouched. Its online brokerage offers low-cost fixed-price trades. Customers with less than $250,000 in investable assets are advised by its financial advisory call center. With up to $1 million in assets, the customer gets a financial advisor. Wealth management advisors handle the up-to-$10 million crowd. And private banking and investment professionals take on the job of advising those who have $10 million or more socked away.

Global Private Client recruits undergrads and MBA candidates for its analyst and associate programs. These programs usually start the summer before your final year of school; Merrill makes offers for its 2-year program based on summertime performance. Analysts typically work out of corporate campuses in Princeton, Hopewell, and Jersey City, New Jersey. Some get placed in the Big Apple. As an analyst or associate, you'll work in one of five areas that generally support Merrill's network of financial advisors: private banking and investment, retirement, consumer banking, the financial advisor call center, and investments and wealth management. Support might mean helping create investment products or creating a marketing campaign. It doesn't mean selling bonds to Florida grannies, nor does it mean just running spreadsheet models. "We don't want individuals to sit at a cube all day and crunch numbers but to create a marketing campaign and analyze it, sell it," says an insider.

MORGAN STANLEY

1585 Broadway
New York, NY 10036
Phone: 212-761-4000
Fax: 212-762-0575
www.morganstanley.com

Morgan Stanley's retail brokerage operations came to life via the 1997 merger between Dean Witter Discover, the dining card-cum retail brokerage, and white-shoe investment bank Morgan Stanley. Morgan Stanley dropped Dean Witter from its name in 2002, and its brokerage operations are now the fifth largest in the country. Morgan Stanley offers a range of options to clients, with its focus on the high-net-worth customer. Morgan Stanley's individual investor group, which makes most of its money from commissions and asset management fees charged to its retail brokerage clients, had $602 billion in client assets at the end of November 2004. The number of the group's global representatives has slipped for the past 3 years; it now stands at 10,962 employees. Revenue rose in 2004 by 9 percent to $4.6 billion.

PIPER JAFFRAY COMPANIES

800 Nicollet Mall, Suite 800
Minneapolis, MN 55402
Phone: 612-303-1066 or 800-333-6000
Fax: 612-303-8199
www.piperjaffray.com

Piper Jaffray bucked the trend of consolidation and spun off from its commercial banking parent, U.S. Bancorp, in 2003. The firm splits its business into capital markets and private client services. Capital markets engages in equities and debt underwriting and mergers advisory. Private client services offers investment products and services for individuals and small businesses. In April 2005, Piper created a wealth management group that provides some of the more complicated services that oodles of dough necessitate, such as estate planning, philanthropy management, and wealth transfer.

The Minneapolis-based firm has 111 offices in 23 states and London and employs more than 3,000. Revenue from its private client group rose a modest 0.9 percent to $355 million in 2004. When recruiting for its financial advisor and financial advisor associate positions, Piper prefers people with experience in other professions to recent college grads. New brokers first go through a 5- to 6-month training program that includes registration and compliance, product knowledge, and portfolio management skills. Compensation, which is partly salary and partly derived from the clients' assets and activity, should be in the low six figures by the fourth year.

RAYMOND JAMES & ASSOCIATES, INC.

880 Carillon Parkway
St. Petersburg, FL 33716
Phone: 727-567-1000
Fax: 727-567-8915
www.raymondjames.com/rja

From the sunny shores of Florida, Raymond James has spread its financial advisory services to 2,200 locations worldwide, including affiliates in Argentina and Turkey. Its slogan, "Individual solutions from independent advisors," refers to its network of financial advisors, who can fall into one of five employment categories: traditional employee, independent, independent contractor, fee-only firm and bank/credit union. Each of these models gives employees different levels of autonomy and has a different fee and payment structure. As an "independent employee," for instance, a financial advisor establishes his or her own branch office. Raymond James handles the human resources, payroll, technology and administrative support for the office. Not surprisingly, the firm stresses that it has kept up-to-date with the latest technology for clearing and custody services.

To get a position in a Raymond James financial advisor training program, you generally have to have a bachelor's degree and the ability to obtain a Series 7 license within 90 days. The training program lasts 28 months and rewards its charges with salary, commissions, and other incentive compensation. Of course, its main goal is to prepare advisors to set up shop. Raymond James financial advisors number more than 4,800; the firm has $136 billion in client assets.

SMITH BARNEY PRIVATE CLIENT GROUP

388 Greenwich Street
New York, NY 10013
Phone: 212-816-6000 or 800-EARNS-IT
Fax: 212-793-9086
www.smithbarney.com

Smith Barney Private Client Group today comprises one-third of Citigroup's Global
Wealth Management Group; Citigroup Private Bank and Smith Barney Equity
Research make up the remainder. With roots stretching back to the 19th century and a
history packed with brokerage mergers, Smith Barney Private Client today claims more
than 12,100 financial consultants and 500 offices. Its 7.5 million client accounts have
sunk $978 billion into the operation.

Sister unit Smith Barney Equity Research recruits from the college crowd. But the brokerage looks for more experienced professionals when it comes to financial consultants.
Applicants should have at least 5 years of business experience and at least a bachelor's
degree. Successful candidates for the financial advisory program typically start in a 36-
month paid training program.

TD WATERHOUSE GROUP, INC.

100 Wall Street, 28th Floor
New York, NY 10005
Phone: 212-806-3500 or 800-934-4448
Fax: 212-785-1636
www.tdwaterhouse.com

You may know TD Waterhouse by the craggy features of *Law & Order* star Sam Waterston, who's been trying to coax customers of full-service brokers to the discount broker. A subsidiary of Canada's Toronto-Dominion Bank, TD Waterhouse has 3.2 million active accounts and $172 billion in assets. Besides its online presence, investors can visit its 140 offices nationwide.

The firm is no stranger to deals, but it narrowly avoided a big one last year when its parent and rival E-Trade broke off talks of a merger. Like its peers, TD Waterhouse has tweaked its model to be a bit more hands-on than a pure discount brokerage. In a bid to hang onto customers once their increased wealth puts them on the radar screen for the private banks and wealth managers, it's been asking customers to fill out question-naires. Based on the answers, it may refer the client to a registered investment advisor.

UBS FINANCIAL SERVICES INC.

1285 Avenue of the Americas
New York, NY 10019
Phone: 212-713-2000
Fax: 212-713-9818
financialservicesinc.ubs.com

One of the largest banks in the world, UBS became a major force in retail brokerage when it purchased Paine Webber. In the United States, UBS helps individuals invest their money through its UBS Financial Services broker/dealer. UBS has in its ranks 7,500 registered financial representatives who work out of 366 offices nationwide. UBS brokers spend much of their time calling on wealthy clients or taking the really wealthy ones out to lunch. Additionally, advisors are moving their customers to a fee-based, rather than transaction-based, model. That shouldn't be too hard for UBS's financial advisors, who receive 2 years of training.

UBS will accept brokers with a bachelor's degree; however, it prefers candidates with at least 5 years of work experience and really likes those with MBAs, JDs, or CFAs—people who can command respect from potential investors. UBS offers a base salary to new advisors until they have completed the second stage of their training.

WACHOVIA SECURITIES, LLC

901 East Byrd Street
Richmond, VA 23219
Phone: 804-649-2311
Fax: 804-782-3540
www.wachoviasec.com

Formed by the merger of the brokerage groups of Wachovia Bank and Prudential Securities, Wachovia Securities instantly became the country's third-largest retail brokerage in 2003 and is affiliated with the fifth-largest bank. Unlike its parent Wachovia Corp., the brokerage's 3,800 locations and more than 8,000 financial advisors are spread throughout the United States. It has about $650 billion in client assets.

Currently Wachovia hires entry-level positions as brokerage operations specialists on an as-needed basis. But in 2005–06 it hopes to initiate a financial advisor training program that will recruit recent graduates. "We're looking to build a more diverse brokerage unit," says one insider. That means it's looking for women and minorities, as well as young people in general, as it tries to deepen its talent pool.

Additional Asset Management Companies

Though the number of asset management companies and mutual fund advisors are legion, the following companies, though not the largest in the industry, are among the better known and offer ample opportunities for the job seeker.

A I M MANAGEMENT GROUP INC.

11 Greenway Plaza, Suite 100
Houston, TX 77046
Phone: 713-626-1919 or 800-959-4246
Fax: 713-993-9890
www.aimfunds.com

Founded in 1976, A I M has strategically acquired its way to a global presence. It employs more than 2,078 people through its offices in Houston, Denver, and San Francisco. A I M manages 72 retail funds and ten institutional funds, among other investment portfolios. A I M Distributors underwrites the funds. The firm sells funds under the AIM and INVESCO brands. A I M Management is a subsidiary of AMVESCAP, a British company. The firm has $131 billion in assets under management.

AMERICAN CENTURY INVESTMENT MANAGEMENT

4500 Main Street, Suite 1500
Kansas City, MO 64111
Phone: 816-531-5575 or 800-345-2021
Fax: 816-340-7962
www.americancentury.com

American Century Investment Management is a diversified family of funds. Started in 1958, it was one of the first to use a computer in portfolio management. Its 80 funds now range from conservative income to aggressive growth. Through reciprocal agreements, American Century is also able to market 11,000 funds from 250 firms. The firm, which is part owned by J.P. Morgan Chase, has roughly $95 billion under management.

American Century employs about 2,000 people and has offices in Kansas City; Denver; Mountain View, California; New York; Singapore; and London. For the past 6 years, it's appeared on *Fortune*'s list of the 100 "Best Companies to Work For."

THE DREYFUS CORPORATION

200 Park Avenue
New York, NY 10166
Phone: 212-922-6000 or 888-271-4994
Fax: 212-922-7533
www.dreyfus.com

The Dreyfus Corporation, established in 1951, has been a subsidiary of Mellon Bank since 1994. Headquartered in New York City, Dreyfus manages more than $161 billion in assets in more than 200 mutual fund portfolios nationwide and is known for its Dreyfus Premier family of equity and bond funds. Originally a bond shop, Dreyfus can now claim that equity funds comprise about 30 percent of its assets under management versus 10 percent when Mellon bought the company. It's also been selling more products through third parties like financial planners than direct to the investors. In 2002, the company sold its online brokerage unit, Brown & Co., to J.P. Morgan Chase and a year later bought Ashland Management.

GABELLI ASSET MANAGEMENT, INC.

1 Corporate Center
Rye, NY 10580
Phone: 914-921-5100 or 800-422-3554
Fax: 914-921-5392
www.gabelli.com

Named after founder Mario Gabelli, Gabelli Asset Management (which wants to change is name to GAMCO) is known for its value-oriented style of investing. It manages mutual funds and offers separate accounts for high-net-worth individuals, institutions, and qualified pension plans, providing advisory services to approximately 30 funds and 1,700 high-net-worth individuals. The company has nearly $30 billion in assets under management. Bill Gates owns a stake of it.

An acolyte of Warren Buffett, the gregarious Mario believes in observing what's going on in society to help make investment decisions. He likes to hire PhDs because they're "poor, hungry, driven people."

JANUS CAPITAL GROUP INC.

151 Detroit Street
Denver, CO 80206
Phone: 303-333-3863
Fax: 303-336-7497
www.janusfunds.com

Janus Capital has seen turmoil in recent years. First, the publicly traded firm reorganized and merged with its parent company Stillwell Financial in 2003. Around that time, Janus admitted to engaging in market timing activities. Add to that the tumultuous fate of technology stocks, in which Janus tended to have large positions, and you end up with a less-than-rosy predicament. In August 2004, it reached a $226 million final settlement with regulators over market-timing charges.

Janus currently has $132 billion in assets under management, a big drop from its peak. Besides its flagship Janus Capital Management, the firm owns institutional quantitative manager INTECH and 30 percent of value investor Perkins, Wolf, McDonnell & Co. As it tries to put bad publicity behind it, Janus has tweaked its compensation structure for managers so that they're rewarded more for performance than growth in assets. Plus, new management has fleshed out analyst coverage so Janus' investments are decidedly less tech-heavy.

LAZARD ASSET MANAGEMENT

30 Rockefeller Plaza, 57th Floor
New York, NY 10112
Phone: 800-821-6474
www.lazardnet.com

One of the main divisions of 157-year-old European-American investment bank Lazard, Lazard Asset Management invests assets for individuals and institutions in the United States, Britain, Germany, Australia, and Japan, plus serves as an adviser to several mutual fund families. Under the direction of Wall Street dealmaker Bruce Wasserstein, parent Lazard made its IPO debut in Spring 2005—thus promising that a few of the secretive institution's mysteries would make the light of day.

NEUBERGER BERMAN INC.

605 Third Avenue
New York, NY 10158
Phone: 212-476-9000
Fax: 212-476-9090
www.nb.com

Since 1939, when the company was founded, Neuberger Berman has been striving to make the wealthy even wealthier. The company's namesake and founder, Roy Neuberger, was an art patron and investor who founded the company to cater to individuals like himself. The firm, which is now part of Lehman Brothers, manages more than 40 mutual funds for institutions and individuals and offers financial advisory services to both client segments. In keeping with its focus on the blue-blood set, it offers separate accounts for clients that have $10 million in assets or more. Neuberger Berman has $88.5 billion in assets under management and employs 108 portfolio managers who have a combined average industry experience of 23 years.

OPPENHEIMERFUNDS, INC.

2 World Financial Center
225 Liberty Street
New York, NY 10281
Phone: 212-323-0200
Fax: 212-323-4070
www.oppenheimerfunds.com

A subsidiary of MassMutual, OppenheimerFunds—not to be confused with
Oppenheimer & Co.—has been in the investment management business since 1960.
Today, the company is one of the largest mutual fund companies in the United States,
offering 60 funds and managing $170 billion in client assets. The company has
expanded its services to include variable annuities and qualified retirement funds. It's
also the parent of hedge fund firm Tremont Capital Management.

T. ROWE PRICE GROUP, INC.

100 East Pratt Street
Baltimore, MD 21202
Phone: 410-345-2000
Fax: 410-345-2394
www.troweprice.com

Started in 1937, T. Rowe Price today manages $235 billion in client assets for individ-
uals, corporations, and institutions. Known for its growth style of investing, or finding
companies whose earnings and dividends look like they'll grow faster than inflation
and the overall economy, T. Rowe's fund performances have helped it reel in assets. Its
Capital Appreciation Fund in 2004 was the only U.S. equity fund to post positive
returns 14 years in a row, even through the most recent and quite severe bear market.

The Baltimore-based firm also has offices in Amsterdam, Buenos Aires, Copenhagen,
Hong Kong, London, Paris, Singapore, and Tokyo.

On the Job

The Big Picture

Portfolio Management and Research Roles

Broker/Advisor Roles

Support Roles

Real People Profiles

The Big Picture

Whether you're a "quant jock" who salivates like Pavlov's dog when you see a spreadsheet, or a social animal who jumps out of your seat to meet new people and build relationships, or even that rare beast who is both quantitative and social, the retail brokerage and asset management industries have fulfilling and lucrative opportunities to satisfy your yen.

Though many of the roles in the brokerage and asset management industries are similar, you can split these unsplittable industries in a few key ways. Asset management companies tend to have customers that are institutional investors and some wealthy individuals, whereas retail brokerages primarily serve individuals. Roles in asset management companies are typically considered "buy-side"; that is, they are within companies that trade securities or analyze stocks for their own portfolios. Roles in the retail brokerage industry tend to be "sell-side," or within companies that trade or analyze stocks for clients that engage in trading.

Asset management companies, including hedge and mutual funds, are in the business of increasing the wealth of their constituent investors through the management of a pool of funds. Leading this endeavor is the fund manager, who executes the strategy of the fund and directs investments. Supporting the fund manager is a group of analysts. Analysts evaluate industries and the stocks and bonds issues within them. Bond analysts tend to be more technical and quantitative than stock analysts. Analysts often reside within a research group and work for multiple fund managers. Unlike analysts at securities firms, they also tend to evaluate stocks across industries. Also within the research department are a small number of economists and investment strategists who do very high-level strategy—they try to predict the direction of the economy and markets and come up with general portfolio strategies accordingly. Because they often deal in high volumes or very specialized securities, asset managers also have in-house trading groups to manage the positions of a particular fund or group of funds. Asset managers also have a front-end team, a sales and relationship management team to find new investors, manage the accounts of existing investors, and, in the case of some direct-distribution mutual funds, market to the general public. Behind them is an array of support staff that includes financial analysts who do fund accounting, operations specialists who do trade settlement, compliance officers who ensure that employees are not engaging in insider trading or other illicit activities, and, in the case of mutual funds that deal directly with the public, customer service agents.

Retail brokerage firms tend to be slices of larger securities firms that also engage in institutional brokerage and investment banking. This guide focuses on roles within the retail portion of these companies. At the heart of retail brokerage firms are, astonishingly, brokers or financial advisors. Brokers not only execute securities trades for their clients and advise them on individual issues or mutual funds, they also help align their portfolios and in some cases, offer clients other financial products such as life insurance. Many retail brokerages have special departments for their wealthy clients, the financial services industry's equivalent of a casino's high-roller room. These private banking or private client services groups, as they are known in the industry, offer wealthy individuals attentive service and a number of nontraditional investment products. Private bankers are sort of the stockbrokers for the rich and famous. Supporting these brokers is a cast of characters similar to those in the asset management industry. Analysts provide recommendations on stocks for brokers to give to their clients; they also consult with a brokerage's traders to keep them informed of company developments that could trigger stock movements. The cast of characters is rounded out by compliance officers and operations, technology, and marketing groups.

You can find a large number of these positions outside of the massive asset management firms and brokerages. There are plenty of independent brokers and research firms. Most of these companies, however, are looking for people who have already earned their stripes in their respective departments of the major brokerage houses and asset management companies.

Finally, if you have spent time in the financial services industry and decide that you're yearning for a firm that makes something other than money, the finance departments at corporations usually welcome refugees from the finance industry with open arms. People making the jump back into corporate finance usually find the best fits as financial analysts and in investor relations.

Portfolio Management and Research Roles

FUND ACCOUNTANT

Salary: $35,000 to $50,000
Education: BA/BS in finance or accounting

As a fund accountant, you have a singular vision: Calculate the net asset value, the price which customers pay, for a mutual fund. You do this by tracking the fund's holding and closing prices for the securities owned as well as income earned and customer withdrawals. The job consists of checking ledger entries, running valuation reports, and recording account transactions.

An accounting or finance degree is a typical requirement. In some firms, the position is seen as a way of learning about the fund industry and portfolio management.

JUNIOR RESEARCH ANALYST

Salary: $60,000 to $100,000
Education: BA/BS

Typically an entry-level position at a firm such as Goldman or Merrill, this prized role does the bidding of the equity analyst. The role includes reading 10-Ks to find new company information, updating and maintaining financial models, synthesizing and analyzing external company and industry data, proofreading PowerPoint presentations and research reports, conducting primary research by calling industry contacts, and writing minor research reports and analyst notes. The role is essentially the assistant to an analyst or group of analysts. However, it brings you incredible exposure within the company and sets you up in an analyst track. Most junior analysts get MBAs and continue in the industry as associates, then senior analysts, and eventually managing director. Junior analyst roles are entry level or require 1 to 2 years of experience.

Many firms look for people with accounting or finance degrees. However, top firms such as Credit Suisse will take college graduates from a wide range of majors, as long as they have excellent quantitative and communications skills.

QUANTITATIVE ANALYST

Salary: $100,000-plus
Education: MS, PhD

Black hole physics got you down? Tired of trying to make cocktail party conversation with your game theory dissertation and bringing home dates to your shared apartment with milk-crate bookshelves? If there was ever a place for physics and math PhDs to become as wealthy as Croesus, it's as a quantitative analyst.

Quantitative analysts typically develop computer models to value securities and structure portfolios that are used in portfolio management and program trading. The position usually requires programming skills such as C or Java in addition to superior analytical skills and good communication skills—you have to meet with clients as well. Prospective candidates usually don't have to have previous finance experience for this position—firms will train you in portfolio theory, valuation, and securities regulation. They'll assume you'll be a quick study; though you aren't necessarily an Einstein, you are very likely a rocket scientist.

ECONOMIST

Salary: $65,000 to $150,000
Education: BA/BS, MS/MA, PhD

Are you a budding Alan Greenspan, but want a piece of the action now? Economists sit in both buy-side and sell-side companies. As an economist, you typically provide an opinion on the future of the market and general economy based on models that you develop and maintain, third-party models and analysis, and analysis of global and domestic news and economic indicators. You communicate your position on the economy and the market through written analysis briefs and meetings with internal clients—analysts and portfolio managers.

BUY-SIDE RESEARCH ANALYST

Salary: $150,000 to $1 million (for the big Wall Street firms)
Education: BA/BS, MBA
Credential: CFA

Fixed-income analysts typically work in small teams, up to a dozen analysts, that perform credit analysis of individual securities and analysis of the overall market. Analysts in generally usually support a portfolio manager but report to a director within the research department. The analyst's product is a recommendation—buy, sell, or hold—of a security to a fund manager. Additionally, analysts come up with investing ideas for portfolio managers based on their research. Analysts spend most of their time analyzing the cash flows of the companies underlying the securities they are evaluating, researching economic and social trends to understand the direction of interest rates, talking to analysts at credit rating agencies such as Moody's (for fixed-income securities) or to sell-side analysts at brokerage firms to better understand the securities and the market, and presenting their recommendations and findings to fund managers.

The role typically requires an MBA in finance, work toward a CFA, and significant quantitative abilities.

SELL-SIDE RESEARCH ANALYST

Salary: $150,000 to $1 million-plus
Education: BA/BS, MBA
Credential: CFA

Research analysts are a little like real-life doctors who play doctors on television; they have all the skills, training, and experience required of their profession and, on top of that, they have a public presence and communication skills that would put Dale Carnegie to shame. Brokerage firms put their analysts in the spotlight, helping them get spots on CNBC or *MoneyTalk*; their reputation adds luster and brand recognition to the firm. Not all analysts are this high profile, but all must do their share of media snippets and conferences. The equity research position is not a role for the shy or the tongue-tied. Research analysts evaluate equities in a given industry, as well as the industry itself. With the financial models they develop, and through data they collect from 10-Ks, analyst calls, meetings with industry executives, and general industry knowledge, research analysts recommend (or pan) stocks and give opinions about where they think the industry is headed; they do this for both internal and external clients.

It's important to note that research teams are generally cost centers in brokerages. They don't generate revenue on their own, but rather support investment bankers and traders by giving them briefings on equities, and in the past, touted stocks of investment banking clients to goose I-banking sales.

PORTFOLIO MANAGER

Salary: $200,000 to $1 million-plus
Education: BA/BS, often MBA
Credentials: CFA

The previous rung on the career ladder for most portfolio managers is investment or research analyst, or possibly junior portfolio manager. After passing on your stock picking analysis to the bloke running the fund, you have the chance to make your own calls. As a portfolio manager you're at the pinnacle of the asset management world. At some level, the job is pretty straightforward: Your company, be it a mutual fund, pension fund, or other fund, has specific investment goals, and your job is to pick a portfolio of stocks, bonds, or combination of the two, to make the highest returns for investors given those goals. The job is analytical, strategic, and on some level, sales oriented.

All of the following might be part of a day: You order traders to execute the purchase or sale of securities. You meet with the CEO of a company you're thinking of investing in to grill him about the business. You huddle with your assistant manager or analysts to go over stock picks, optimization of short-term instruments like money market securities, and your fund's alpha rating. You then work with them to tweak the financial model that's the basis of your day-to-day fund management. You spend some time getting briefed on industry developments and corporate intelligence. Add to that client-relations work. If you are managing a pension or other asset fund, you might brief a charitable foundation on your investing strategy for a sales call or meet with the investment manager of a current client to review your fund's performance.

Broker/Advisor Roles

Retail brokerage and financial advisory are sales. Although you advise people on the best way to invest their wealth, you're in the business of getting people to buy your financial services products, be they stock transactions, life insurance, mutual funds, or portfolio planning. It's important to know this when considering the profession—to be successful you need to be a good salesperson, networking, building trust, and getting sales. In the institutional world, you are still performing sales, but your clients are brokerage firms or banks that you are trying to get to carry your fund, institutions whose money you are trying to invest, or corporations whose assets you are trying to manage.

STOCKBROKER ASSISTANT

Salary: $30,000 to $50,000
Credentials: Series 7, 63

A stockbroker assistant performs many of the administrative tasks for a stockbroker, such as calling clients to confirm trades, attending to client requests, and performing reporting. After you've secured your Series 7 license, you become actively engaged in explaining products to clients, opening new accounts, and eventually executing trades. In a good firm, the broker assistant position represents an excellent way to become licensed and learn the business.

STOCKBROKER/FINANCIAL ADVISOR

Salary: $75,000 to $1 million-plus
Education: BA/BS; MBA, JD, or MD preferred
Credentials: Series 7, 63

As you'd expect, stock brokerage and financial advisory are sales roles, but this isn't selling Clinique at the cosmetics counter. Your job is to acquire new clients, then sell them a variety of products, from stock recommendations and mutual funds, to annuity-based life insurance. In the world of wealth management, you're getting people who are hard-working and smart enough to stock up hundreds of thousands or even millions of dollars to entrust you with their life savings.

Accordingly, many brokerage firms aren't looking for pimply-faced kids who are still holding a beer bong to fill the ranks of the financial advisory and stock brokerage practices. Typically, firms recruit people with significant life experience and professional accomplishments. Merrill Lynch, for instance, looks for people with at least 5 years of professional experience and preferably with a professional degree such as an MD or JD. Other firms, such as Edward Jones, hire undergraduates. Still the experience serves two purposes: It gives people a sense that they are dealing with someone who is mature and, even more important, it gives you a few years to build up a network of high earner contacts from med or law school. Most brokerages give their financial advisors significant training. In addition to Series 7 (the license required to sell securities) training, firms give up to 5 years of ongoing training in stock market basics, investment planning, asset allocation, and sales.

Compensation structures vary greatly among firms in the industry, but incentive-based pay is typical. Charles Schwab pays based on revenue products from the broker's client assets under management, and making more than $150,000 a year is not unrealistic. Edward Jones pays entirely on commission after a year of training and ramp-up. Most firms will pay you a base salary until you build up a clientele, after which your salary is often entirely commission-based.

Stock brokering is not for the faint of heart. In addition to offering income that's based solely on your performance and spiced by overall economic conditions, it's grueling until you build up your client base. Piper Jaffray expects that for the first 3 to 5 years, 50- to 60-hour workweeks are the norm. And you have to be ready for rejection. One insider reports the following statistics in prospecting for clients: "You might make 100 calls to clients. Of those calls you might actually get to leave a message or talk to someone 25 percent of the time. From there, you might get a callback from or talk to 15 people. Of those, you might schedule two or three initial advisory sessions—prospects."

Just like any other sales job, you have to do a lot of cold-calling and play the numbers game when you are starting out. And you have to have pretty thick skin. When you're starting out, you might be making 100 to 150 calls a day. An insider says, "It can get pretty discouraging. I make a plan for myself: I make perhaps 15 or 20 calls. I get called all sorts of names by some people; it can get brutal. I then walk away and do something else for a half-hour and start up again."

PRIVATE BANKER/PRIVATE CLIENT SERVICES

Salary: $150,000 to $1 million-plus
Education: MBA
Credentials: Series 7, 63

Private bankers are like financial advisors on steroids. They offer financial services and advice to wealthy individuals and earn wads of cash for their efforts. Their profile can range from a bank-branch employee schooled in some products that might interest folks with more than $250,000 in investing assets to brokerage wealth managers catering to families with more than $500 million in assets; these bankers are often highly specialized and carry multiple degrees. Private banking units usually charge their clients a fee for their services based on a percentage of assets under management. So the more assets a client brings to the institution, the sweeter the payout to the banker, who receives a percentage of these fees over time for her hard work.

As with quotidian financial advisory, private bankers have to build their own clientele, and a wealthy one at that. Private client-services brokers often find themselves living the jet-set life of their clients. One insider reports having to take his client to the Masters tournament in Augusta and later meeting another client, a casino entrepreneur, in Las Vegas.

As with mere financial advisors, private bankers typically have at least 5 years of professional experience as well as professional degrees such as MDs and JDs. A law degree is particularly attractive the further up the wealth ladder one goes, since understanding legalese comes in handy when helping clients in areas like estate planning. Aside from hiring well-connected people, private banks recruit relatively heavily from MBA programs. Although you still need to be connected, MBA recruiting affords an entrée into private client services that you might not otherwise have had.

WHEN PETER MET LEXI

As an undergrad at Columbia University, Peter Bacanovic met Alexis Stewart. Through Alexis he also met Martha. Fast-forward a few years. When he became a stockbroker at Merrill Lynch, Pierce, Fenner & Smith, Peter Bacanovic no doubt told Martha about his new job and how he might be able to help her. Martha took him up on the offer—after all, she had known him for years.

This story illustrates two things: First, to be successful in private banking, you need to have to have a Rolodex with a few impressive names, or at least be only a degree or two of separation removed from them. Second, you have to be able to gain the trust of people who are not only fabulously wealthy, but among the most powerful individuals in their fields. It's not a business for the meek or for the isolated.

INSTITUTIONAL RELATIONSHIP MANAGER

Salary: $100,000 to $175,000
Education: BA/BS, MBA
Credential: Series 7, 63

Relationship managers ensure that institutional clients of mutual funds or other institutional products are happy; they resolve issues, educate clients on products, and implement new processes. Relationship managers also advise and sell clients new products. Typically, relationship managers deal with large institutions and do so at a senior executive level. Usually, this is a midcareer position.

INSTITUTIONAL SALES MANAGER

Salary: $150,000 to $500,000
Education: BA/BS, MBA
Credential: Series 7, 63

Sales managers call on pension funds, union plans, banks, and other institutional clients and sell them funds, back-office products, or other products. They usually operate on a territory model, prospecting for new clients and selling add-on products to existing customers in a specified geography. The job involves some travel, sometimes up to 50 percent, which is high for the financial services industry. It also involves some cold-calling and a lot of networking, particularly with the fund consultants who act as a middle-man between the pension plans and companies that manage funds. Some firms expect sales reps to generate up to 20 warm leads (in-person presentations) a month. Often, sales managers have telesales staffs to help prospect for new clients. Once at a client presentation, you'll pitch your fund with a product team. It's also a midcareer hire. Those with aspirations in this potentially very lucrative business often start as traders or analysts, since knowing the industry backward and forward is key.

Support Roles

COMPLIANCE OFFICER

Salary: $40,000 to $150,000
Education: BA/BS

Compliance groups police securities and investment firms to prevent company employees from violating SEC regulations. Roles in compliance usually start at the analyst level and move up to vice president. Compliance officers set up "Chinese Walls," or barriers between different groups in the company to prevent the spread of insider trading; monitor communications to prevent insider information from spreading outside the firm or between groups; track trades of employees to ensure that they aren't buying or selling "gray list" securities; work with different company groups to establish gray lists or lists of clients that the firm is working with and on which the firm may have insider information; and develop the policies and procedures of the group along with company attorneys and external regulators.

CUSTOMER SERVICE

Salary: $25,000 to $45,000
Education: BA/BS

If you're determined to get into the asset management or brokerage industries and all else fails, you could look for a position in a customer service department. Here, you help customers understand their transactions, read their statements, and help them with product information. The role gives you a grounding in the industry and the company. Customer service agents typically need Series 7 and 63 licenses, which firms will often sponsor.

Real People Profiles

MUTUAL FUND PORTFOLIO MANAGER

Years in business: 7

Age: 38

Education: BA in history, MBA

Hours per week: 50 to 55

Size of company: 500 employees

Certification: not required

Annual salary: more than $200,000

What do you do?

I manage a stock fund whose exclusive investor is a large pension fund; it's not for mom-and-pop investors. My fund specializes in telecommunications stocks. I pick the stocks we buy and sell, and it's my job to be familiar with the industry as a whole, analyze particular companies, and meet with the management of the companies we invest in. I do a lot of modeling and projections, but I also have to do some marketing and press relations.

How did you get your job?

I got my job by working in the industry for a while and getting to know lots of people. I got my first mutual fund job through the career center at Stanford, where I got my MBA. After several years in the industry, I'd made a lot of connections, and I got head-hunted for my current position.

What are your career aspirations?

Ten years from now, I want to be doing something very similar to what I'm doing now: managing money, researching new companies, and so on. The excitement of working in mutual funds is not in changing jobs, but staying abreast of the changes in the markets and the economy generally.

What kinds of people do really well at this business?

People who think in webs do well at picking stocks. You have to be intellectually curious, and you have to be able to synthesize ideas. If you know A equals B, and B equals C, then you have to figure out that A equals C, too. You have to be able to make connections, but the connections aren't always obvious.

What do you really like about your job?

My job is like a window on the world. To be good, you have to keep up with a constantly changing world. In the telecommunications industry, there's always a whole new set of companies to learn about. And the stock market is like a daily jolt of adrenaline, whether it goes up or down.

What do you dislike?

I live on the West Coast, so I have to get up really early if I want to follow the markets in New York. Also, you're bound to make mistakes—pick the wrong stocks—and it can be painful when you're wrong, even if you learn something in the process. This business is humbling.

What is the biggest misconception about this job?

People often don't understand what I do. People who don't know finance think it's like being a banker. They don't understand the rapidity of the changes a mutual fund manager deals with. Basically, they don't understand how exciting it can be.

How can someone get a job like yours?

An MBA is the most useful route to becoming a fund manager. People should also be willing to take a job beneath their talents when they start out. If you show good judgment, you can advance rapidly, so be willing to take whatever offer comes your way. You've also got to be willing to relocate to a big city.

Describe a typical day.

7:00   Have to get in early so I can watch the market. Get to my desk, skim the *Wall Street Journal*, and check my e-mails and voice mails. In particular, I want to check to make sure transactions from the previous day were completed.

8:00   Attend a regular meeting with other portfolio managers for a general discussion of the market, plus discussion of specific stocks. People recommend specific articles in the *Wall Street Journal*, that kind of thing.

9:15   Start reading the mass of information on my desk. I'm a slow reader, but I know how to skim for the necessary information quickly.

10:30   Place phone calls to management of several different companies we're thinking of investing in to fill in gaps in our research and get more of a feel for the company.

11:30   Call securities analysts at a couple of brokerage firms to pick their brains about certain stocks.

12:00   Lunch at my desk.

12:30   Prepare for a meeting with management from a company we're thinking of investing in. Look over their numbers and prepare questions.

1:00   Meet with representatives from the company. They make a brief presentation introducing the company, and then I ask questions about financial ratios, future plans, and overall competitive strategy.

2:00   Talk informally with some of the people I manage, including analysts and researchers. We talk about various stocks. I ask their opinions on some companies I'm studying.

2:30   Prepare for a meeting with another company we're thinking of investing in.

3:00   The meeting proceeds very much like the previous one.

4:00   Have to make a marketing call to a huge potential investor explaining the investment goals of our fund.

4:30   Go back to my reading, which includes company press releases, IPO docu-
       ments, our own analyses, and analyses from the sell side (i.e., brokerage
       houses). Meanwhile, check to see how the market has performed, especially the
       stocks we own.

6:30   Call it a day.

MUTUAL FUND INVESTMENT ANALYST

Years in business: 4
Age: 33
Education: BA, MBA
Hours per week: 50 to 60
Size of company: 2,000 employees
Certification: Chartered Financial Analyst
Annual salary: $250,000

What do you do?

As an analyst, I cover the business services and transportation industries. I also coman-
age a midcap stock fund, which specializes in companies worth between $1 billion and
$8 billion. I do financial modeling, meet with company management, and in general
perform strategic assessments of both companies and industries. As a portfolio manager, I also make decisions about asset allocation—exactly how much money we're
going to invest and where.

How did you get your job?

I got my job through on-campus recruiting at UCLA's business school. A UCLA alum
who manages a fund at my firm placed the ad. I probably stood out because I had experience in business valuation; I'd done M&A-type work with Peat Marwick (now part of
KPMG) and Merrill Lynch. I was also singularly focused on getting into the industry.
Being an interviewer myself, I can tell who really wants to get into the industry.

What are your career aspirations?

Basically, I want to be doing what I'm doing now. Hopefully, I'll be managing a larger fund, perhaps one with $500 million or $1 billion in assets. I'm definitely interested in growth as opposed to value investing, so I'd like that to be my focus.

What kinds of people do really well at this business?

You should have a driving curiosity. You should have the instincts of a detective—the desire to turn over every stone so you can find out information that other people might not have. You also have to be a self-starter. Your only deliverable is your own opinions, so it's up to you to form them.

What do you really like about your job?

There's huge independence with this work. Plus, you have a lot of high-level contacts. I met with the CEO of Starbucks today, for example. I also like the focus on strategy. There's no right answer, so you pit your best guess against that of others. You have the potential to earn lots of money, and you're surrounded by people with lots of brainpower.

What do you dislike?

Sometimes there's less human interaction than I'd like. You spend a lot of time poring over numbers: SEC documents and company reports. And of course like everywhere, there are company politics. But I'd say they're both minor points overall.

What is the biggest misconception about this job?

You're not just crunching numbers, which is what most people think. There's a lot of strategizing, and that requires personal assessment of companies and industries. You make lots of qualitative assessments, too, assessing not just sales and profits but also management styles, for example.

How can someone get a job like yours?

First of all, you should be literate with numbers. You also have to demonstrate that driving curiosity. There are very few positions, so candidates who know the industry well are definitely going to stand out. Do the research. You might also consider getting a CFA [Certified Financial Advisor] certificate. It'll show you're serious about the industry.

Describe a typical day.

7:00   As soon as I get in, check quotes for the previous day's biggest gainers and losers, just to make sure there are no disasters. Then I read the *Wall Street Journal* and scan for any stories about companies we're invested in. Then I listen to about 15 voice mails from brokers who may have tips or other trade information to convey.

9:00   Head to our daily departmental meeting. Basically, we just swap ideas, share major news items—that kind of thing. People throw out their daily tidbits.

9:30   Have to prepare for a lunch meeting with a company we're considering investing in. Pore over annual reports, SEC documents, and other data and analyses.

11:30   The company's representatives arrive and start their "road show," which is basically them pitching their company to us. They're trying to convince us they're a good investment. Lunch is served, so we're eating and taking notes at the same time. It's kind of like being in school, except we're not just students but also judge and jury.

1:30   Head back to my office and write down some thoughts about the company. Basically, I have to decide whether it's a worthwhile investment and then make my recommendation. So it takes some time and thought.

3:00   Consult with a sell-side analyst at Merrill Lynch. We compare notes on a couple of companies we're both studying. Since they're on the sales side, they're generous with their research in the hopes of generating a sale.

4:00   Take an hour to talk with a few executives at another company we're considering investing in. They're opening a new division, and I want to find out what their plan is and how it fits with their overall company strategy.

5:00   Spend the last part of my day doing research on a number of different companies. Fine-tune some financial models I've been working on, and then go over some models from the sell side to make sure they jibe with our own analyses.

6:30   Done for the day. Head to the gym.

RETAIL BROKER

Years in business: 9

Age: 37

Education: BS in civil engineering

Hours per week: more than 40

Size of company: 7,000 consultants nationally, five in my local branch, with a staff of 40

Certification: none

Annual salary: $250,000 to $300,000

What do you do?

In a nutshell, I help retirees and pre-retirees manage their money. I find out what's important to them financially and help them set objectives. I do a lot of analysis and then I put together a five- or six-page document, which lays out the big picture for a client. Once we have a plan, I'll talk to and meet with my clients on a regular basis. I personally review and analyze their portfolios. I'm currently working on a combination of commissions and fees, but will probably be moving toward all fees soon.

How did you get your job?

My mother was the wire operator in the office, and I got to know the people there while I was in high school and college. After a 6-year stint in the Navy, I was offered a job working under a consultant/broker in the office. I trained and worked on my own for about 6 months, then my predecessor retired and gave me his book of clients, which amounted to about two-thirds of my assets at the time. I continued to build my business from there.

What are your career aspirations?

I hope to be doing exactly this for the rest of my career, with a few refinements. I would like my client list to include only clients who I really like and whose business I want. I would like to be able to engineer my time so that I spend most of it doing the activities I enjoy the most, such as meeting with clients and making presentations. And I would like to be supported by a staff who can take care of all the other stuff and who enjoy their part in the process as much as I enjoy mine. Ultimately, I hope to build my business to where I am generating $10 million a year in recurring revenue.

What kinds of people do really well at this business?

You should not be overly analytical, which can lead to "CFP" syndrome—for "can't friggin' produce." If you're an investment genius but have no people skills, you're better off as an analyst. You should be outgoing and personable. Introverts just won't cut it. And you should have a solid work ethic. The first years building a client base can require 70- to 80-hour weeks, and you will have to take anything you can get until you become more established.

What do you really like about your job?

Of course I like the compensation. And I like the exposure I get to all different kinds of great people. I really feel I get to add value to their lives, and I don't just mean financially. I get to know people well and become their grief counselor, their marriage counselor—they'll even come to me for a recommendation on a new car.

What do you dislike?

The worst part is that there's a lot of minutiae, and it's getting worse. Every time some jerk does something to try to rip someone off, another regulation comes about, and we spend a lot of time complying with that stuff. I'm trying to train my staff to take care of more of that.

What is the biggest misconception about this job?

That it's easy money. There is no shortcut. You have to put in a lot of hours and a lot of hard work, especially in the beginning.

How can someone get a job like yours?

You could try to assume my identity and have me assassinated. Other than that, having a military background is seen as good because you get used to working long hours for horrendous pay. You definitely need some kind of work experience, preferably in sales. And you at least need the technical skills required to pass the Series 7, which is fairly mathematical.

Describe a typical day.

7:00   Two days a week are set aside for meetings with clients, making presentations, and generating new contacts. The other days are where I get the office work done. On those days, I spend the first half-hour or so getting oriented. I'll drink coffee (although I'm trying to be good and drink more water), check my e-mail, and mentally prepare for what I need to do that day.

7:30   Talk with my assistant about some regulatory forms that need to be attended to. There seem to be more and more of these things every day.

8:00   Start looking through some client portfolios to evaluate how everything's working. I can spend most of a morning or an entire day doing this.

10:30   My review process is interrupted by a phone call from a client who has a question about a particular investment idea. I tell him I'll look into it and get back to him.

11:00   Have a staff training meeting scheduled, something I've been doing more and more of these days.

12:30   Meet with one of my clients for lunch. Since many of my clients are retirees, they're usually pretty available for lunches.

1:45   Back at the office, I review some of the numbers my assistant has dug up regarding the investment idea my client wanted checked. Look them over and call the client with my opinion. Tell him I think it's a little risky in this market and advise that we stay away from it.

2:15   Resume looking at client portfolios and make some notes about things to change and people to call.

3:00   Put the finishing touches on a presentation I'll be making to a new client the following day. He's about to retire in a year and has lost a lot of money in his 401(k) due to the downturn. He's not in desperate straits, but I'd like to see his money somewhere much safer.

3:30   Head home and mentally prepare for the coming day, which will be full of face-to-face time—the part of the job I like best.

The Workplace

Lifestyle, Hours, and Culture

Workplace Diversity

Travel

Compensation

Vacation, Benefits, and Perks

Career Path

Insider Scoop

Lifestyle, Hours, and Culture

If you're not one of those fortunate enough to have your trust fund managed by a premium asset manager or retail brokerage, the next best thing is to work in the retail brokerage or asset management industry. Though the work is demanding and the hours can be long, especially starting out, insiders are happy to roll in piles of money all day (even if it's someone else's). Aside from very attractive compensation, the industry promises manageable (usually) hours, good vacation, benefits unrivalled by nearly any industry outside of the public sector, and ample challenges.

But you don't have to take our word for it. According to *Fortune* magazine, the asset management and retail brokerage industries are pretty good places to work. Seven of *Fortune*'s "100 Best Companies to Work For" in 2005 are asset managers or retail brokers in one way or another, the same number as in 2004.

If investment banking hours are insane, most investment management jobs are merely crazy. In the make-or-break first few years, you can expect to work 50- to 60-hour weeks or more, and those hours will be action packed. You will probably never have breakfast, lunch, or dinner alone again. There are meetings of every kind where you will keep in touch with the movers and shakers of a particular industry. If you're in retail, there are hundreds of calls to make, clients to schmooze, parties to throw, and hours of research to be done.

As a broker or asset manager, you can expect to be given a high degree of independence in how you spend your time. The flip side is that the weight of building a client base of a winning portfolio falls directly on your shoulders. This means you should be entrepreneurial by nature and able to work creatively in your approach to acquiring clients or beating the S&P 500. If you go into retail brokerage, within 2 or 3 years you will usually have no salary, working entirely for commissions or fees. But if this kind of pressure excites and motivates you, this could be a great career choice.

Best Brokerage and Asset Management Firms to Work For

Rank	Company	Industry
18	Robert W. Baird	Retail brokerage
26	American Century	Asset management
35	Goldman Sachs	Asset management
37	American Express	Retail brokerage
56	A.G. Edwards	Retail brokerage
70	SEI Investments	Asset management
72	Vanguard	Mutual fund management

Source: "100 Best Companies to Work For." *Fortune*, January 24, 2005.

As is often the case when money plays a major role, the industry tends to be on the conservative side. While not as staid as investment banking, the culture that asset management and brokerage professionals work in is relatively formal, especially in client-facing roles. And the higher up the corporate ladder you climb, the more likely it is that you'll be expected to wear a suit every day—a sharp one and, particularly if you're on the East Coast, a black or navy blue one at that. Dress codes and the culture in general tend to loosen up as you move west, especially if you end up in California. The industry is an odd mix of hierarchy and meritocracy, say insiders. But, as always, money talks. And nothing earns respect quite like being a big producer.

Workplace Diversity

The securities industry in general is still dominated by white men, particularly at higher levels of management. A 2003 survey by the Securities Industry Association found that 79 percent of executive managers at surveyed firms were white men, compared to 15 percent white women, 4 percent men of color, and 2 percent for women of color. The biggest showing for women was in lower-level positions: They made up three-fourths of brokers' assistants. For minorities, representation was pretty slim across the board.

That said, certain firms have made a lot of progress promoting women and minorities, with some notable examples. At TIAA-CREF, some 47 percent of staff are minorities. At American Express, women hold 57 percent of managerial and supervisory positions and make up 40 percent of executives and senior managers, according to *Fortune*. Minorities make up 18 percent of senior positions. Meanwhile, at much smaller asset manager American Century, some 49 percent of staff are women. At Vanguard, women account for 47 percent, while at pension manager SEI Investments, some 38 percent are women.

Important to the rising class of young bankers and brokers, there are several executives at the top of the biggest firms who don't fall into the "old white boy" category. Witness Sallie Krawcheck, who was previously CEO of Smith Barney and is now Citigroup's CFO. Stan O'Neal, chairman and CEO of Merrill Lynch, is one of the most powerful African-Americans in corporate America. Adding to that list are Ken Chenault, CEO of American Express; Thomas Jones, CEO of Citigroup's Global Investment Management business; and several high-ranking executives of Indian and Asian descent across the industry. Though the situation is far from perfect, the financial service industry seems intent on promoting talent regardless of color or gender. Indeed, half of Merrill Lynch Global Private Client Group's analyst program is generally made up of women. Success in the industry can be measured in pretty concrete terms; if you make money or your returns are stellar, it's hard to prevent you from getting ahead. The industry also has a reputation for fast-tracking stars. The trip from analyst to managing director can be made in a little more than 10 years—so fasten your seatbelt.

Travel

The extent of travel will depend on your area of expertise in a company. If you're a marketing manager with a company that's opening additional branches or investment centers, you can bet that you'll be on the road most of the time, with long layovers (could be weeks or months) in cities where new openings require splashy promotions. Likewise, if you're a relationship manager or salesperson for a mutual fund or asset management company, you may spend a fair amount of time traveling across the country to see your clients.

For the most part though, travel in the industry is minimal. If you're working the phones, talking to investors on a daily basis, or performing analysis, you're going to stay mostly landlocked, with only an occasional trip for extra training or an incentive vacation. Portfolio managers take short trips to meet company CEOs and get ground-level information on the companies they invest in. And consider this: As a portfolio manager looking at prospective investments, the CEOs are trying to impress you, which makes the travel much more enjoyable. Much to the chagrin of the airlines, people in the industry don't travel to nearly the extent that management consultants do. And that's a good thing.

Compensation

Compensation in the brokerage and asset management industries can be heady. Throughout the industry, compensation is performance-based in one way or another. For portfolio managers and their groups, compensation centers around a lucrative base salary capped by bonuses for fund or company performance. Traders receive bonuses based on how well they execute trades. In the case of stockbrokers, compensation can be 100 percent performance-based. Private bankers who bring in wealthy clients generally receive a percentage of assets, fees, or both, but they might not get that all in one lump sum. In order to encourage bankers to keep clients' assets with the firm, payment for bringing in clients often gets split up over time like an annuity.

RETAIL STOCKBROKERS AND FINANCIAL ADVISORS

Compensation structures in the retail brokerage industry take on a limited number of forms. Broadly speaking, brokers are salaried or receive commission-based compensation. The firms that offer base salary after initial training are limited, by and large, to the discount brokerage and bank financial planning realms.

Traditional brokerage firms, on the other hand, usually pay brokers on a purely commission basis after a specified time or after a period of training. At Edward Jones, the company pays for training and offers a salary of $2,000 a month for 1 year. The broker commission, known as a *payout rate* in the industry, is based on management fees or transaction fees from stock purchases and sales. Typically, a national brokerage firm will pay you 36 to 40 percent of gross fees you earn from your clients. Additionally, the firm will cover expenses such as rent for the office, an administration, local marketing costs, and some office supplies. Independent brokerages offer as high as 90 percent (or higher) payouts to their advisors, but in exchange for this liberty, the advisors have to pay for the entire office infrastructure themselves. For most independent brokers, this brings their payout rate to about the same percentage as that of national brokerages.

The median salary for stockbrokers was slightly more than $125,000 in 2003, owing to a bounce in the stock market, with top performers earning more than double that. Be aware, though, that it's slim pickings until you build a client base. Starting out, you could earn less than $40,000 to $50,000.

MUTUAL FUNDS

The top fund managers of the biggest funds earn basis points on the management fee the fund charges investors, so the more money they manage, the more money they make. Managers of high-performing funds can make $10 million to $15 million a year. Salaries for index fund managers, who maintain funds intended to mirror the performance of a particular market index, usually top out at around $200,000.

HEDGE FUNDS

Hedge fund managers can make some serious bank. According to one hedge fund insider, the average fund manager earns $400,000 per year. In addition to a management fee of 1 to 2 percent of assets, hedge funds tend to take a percentage of profits (should there be any), generally to the tune of 20 percent. So the top hedge fund managers can become quite wealthy. The median starting salary for top MBAs is $100,000.

Asset Management Salaries

Position	Salary Range
Fund manager	$200,000 to >$1 million
Junior analyst	$60,000 to $100,000
Customer representative/back office	$30,000 to $100,000
Compliance officer	$45,000 to $150,000
Fund relationship manager	$100,000 to $175,000
Fund sales	$150,000 to $500,000

Source: WetFeet research.

Vacation, Benefits, and Perks

Asset management and brokerage firms have the distinct advantage of being tied to the Wall Street calendar. The New York Stock Exchange has nine holidays a year; most retail brokerage and asset management firms follow suit. In general, vacation, perquisites, and benefits are excellent in the industry. Vacation varies from as few as 2 weeks to 4 or 5 weeks. Foreign-based companies with significant U.S. operations are especially munificent when it comes to vacation. Asset manager Barclays Global Investors, the San Francisco–based subsidiary of London's Barclays Bank, offers its managing directors 30 vacation and personal days, while principals get 23 days, and associates get 18 days.

Many companies are keenly aware of work/life balance and offer benefits such as flextime, domestic partner benefits, tuition reimbursement, and reimbursement for "life cycle" events such as childbirth classes and home fitness. American Century dangles the carrot of a 4-week paid sabbatical for employees who have served 7 years.

Most companies will also spring for industry training—such as for Series 7 classes and testing. Referral bonus programs are also ubiquitous among top-tier firms. Charles Schwab rewards employees who refer successful job candidates with a $2500 bonus.

Finally, the industry does not forget that it is in the wealth creation business: 401(k) and retirement plans are among the best around. Employer matching in 401(k) programs is ubiquitous. Vanguard's Retirement and Savings Plan allows its "crew" to invest a portion of their income in Vanguard funds and receive additional contributions from the fund giant.

Career Path

OPPORTUNITIES FOR UNDERGRADUATES

Unless you have an uncle who wants to bring you in under his wing, you probably won't get into a retail brokerage trainee program. There are exceptions, however; Edward Jones is noted for bringing undergrads with little work experience into its training program, and Wachovia Securities appears to be planning something similar. Discount brokerages offer opportunities in customer service that can lead to advisory positions. In the majority of asset management firms, you are most likely to get a job involving a lot of phone time with clients, either as an investment service representative or as a salesperson. An industry insider describes his first job out of college as glorified data entry, inputting trades into the computer system. But these positions can help you gain essential product and market knowledge, as well as hone your skills interacting with investors. This experience can position you for a move into management, where you can influence the direction and character of the firm. Those who develop a comprehensive understanding of the whole process and can improve any weak links in the organization will definitely be able to move up. There's no up-or-out policy, and there are opportunities across the board, but sales has the biggest potential for fast advancement.

Some top-tier firms with investment banking operations use that model for undergraduates. Merrill Lynch, for instance, starts recent grads as analysts in its private client group before moving successful employees to other positions in the division. Insiders also recommend doing an investment banking analyst program to get some Wall Street cred (read, analytical skills and industry knowledge) before trying to break into portfolio management.

OPPORTUNITIES FOR MBAS

MBAs will also have a tough time getting into a retail brokerage training program. You may be sharp, but unless you have a few years of solid real-world success behind you (preferably in sales), the brokerage firms don't want to take the risk. At mutual funds, investment counseling firms, and bank trust departments, many MBAs perform research and analysis that contributes to the work of various teams and portfolio managers who are ultimately responsible for the performance of different funds. In some exceptional cases, a talented MBA can sign on as a fund manager, but hot MBAs are more likely to come in as analysts or assistant fund managers. You will gain increasing responsibility as you demonstrate an understanding of the market and make more significant contributions. And, if you're really, really good, there are millions of dollars out there with your name on them.

OPPORTUNITIES FOR MIDCAREER CANDIDATES

In asset management firms, there are more midcareer opportunities in sales, marketing, and administration than in research and portfolio management. Sales, marketing, and administrative skills are more transferable from other industries; analysis and asset management are more specialized, and managers tend to be groomed (not cloned) from within the company.

If you're seeking to get into the retail brokerage industry, success in your first career—be it law, accounting, education, management, sales, or medicine—will give you a huge leg up over a young hotshot MBA. Brokerage firms want maturity, experience, and proven entrepreneurial success.

Insider Scoop

WHAT EMPLOYEES REALLY LIKE

Compensation

Salaries and bonuses in the current market climate aren't setting any records, but then again, not many fund managers are on food stamps. Those who still have jobs are generally well compensated, and when the market turns around, as inevitably it must, Porsche Boxter and "house in the Hamptons"–sized bonuses are sure to return to top portfolio and fund managers. Sales positions can also command hefty bonuses in good times, but nothing like those of I-banking salespeople and traders.

The Challenge

The market has a thousand faces and shows you a new one each day. It can take a lifetime to feel you have any kind of handle on it. Many insiders report that the intellectual challenge—trying to be smarter than the market—keeps their jobs forever interesting. "If you like it, it's a fun game; the smartest people in the world do it," says one insider. "It's like poker except the stakes are a lot bigger." Analysts enjoy the challenge of unraveling a numeric puzzle. And for salespeople, it's all about closing the deal.

Variety of Opportunities

No matter where you start in the asset management business, there are many avenues you can pursue depending on how your interests develop. If marketing is your forte, you can develop and launch new products and services to keep investment dollars coming in. If managing money is your hot button, you can start by doing research and work into an investment management position. You can move from a bank trust department to a mutual fund. You can get into retail brokerage or start your own hedge fund. With a proven ability to make money, there will always be investors willing to pay you to manage theirs.

Less Cutthroat than I-Banking or Consulting

Stability is a quality that most investors desire in an asset management company. Insiders tell us that many asset management companies don't like to lose employees and will create multiple career paths to retain trusted talent. Whereas I-banks have short-term horizons for deals, and consulting firms have similarly time-bound projects, investment counseling firms and mutual fund companies have long-term goals of maintaining their investors' principal and increasing returns with as little risk as possible. These goals translate into a generally more relaxed environment and less of a sink-or-swim mentality. "It's the quality of life," says one insider of a large firm's financial advisor group. "You have the ability to make money and see your family. And it's not the type of environment where you don't have a career path after a few years."

High-Level Contacts

Mutual fund and portfolio managers with a lot of investment money to throw around will find that CEOs of top companies come calling to talk up their operations. Managers, analysts, and researchers have the chance to meet these bigwigs in small, face-to-face meetings and ask them lots of questions that CEOs might otherwise be reluctant to answer. Take notes.

High Visibility

While fame may be too strong a word, top asset managers can attain something like celebrity status within the investment community. If you're well-spoken and stock-savvy, financial news shows and publications will gladly pick your brain on the air or in print—though you might think twice before giving away your biggest trade secrets. You know you're somebody when a caricature of your mug appears on the cover of *Barron's*.

Helping People

When you help people make money, they are very, very appreciative. A lot of people are lost in the wilderness when it comes to financial management, and they're thankful for someone who can show them the way. A retail broker has direct contact with his clients, and close relationships can develop. A mutual fund manager may not meet with John Q. Investor, but a good one never forgets the investors she serves.

WATCH OUT!

Stock Market Volatility

Until recently, there were plenty of professionals out there who had never experienced a real bear market. And now they have. You lose money, your clients lose money, your firm loses money, investors pull out of the market, and ultimately a lot of people lose their jobs. If you're a broker and you have to explain to a client why he may have to postpone retirement for a few years, it's not pretty. If you're one of the unfortunates who gets laid off in a bear market, you may find yourself mixing drinks for your old colleagues until the market turns around. And if you're a savvy fund manager who continues to beat the major indices by just losing less than they are, you may not experience the same satisfaction as you would in a growing market.

Performance Anxiety

Fund or portfolio performance is the key factor for a company's success, and the pressure to perform is high—maybe too high. Hedge funds often update their investors on a monthly or even weekly basis, increasing the chance that a bad spell—even if short—will send assets out the door. "Investors have quick trigger fingers," said one insider.

Investors have so many choices and can make changes to different funds so quickly and cheaply that funds are coming under pressure both to keep costs way down and to beat the market consistently. This can put a lot of pressure on fund managers who are making intelligent bets that can lose no matter how smart they are. Retail brokers are entrusted with the life savings, the retirement plans, the college funds—in short, the dreams—of their clients. If you don't feel that pressure in a bear market, you have ice in your veins.

Internal Competition

Internal competition is not always a negative, but you have to watch out for the degree to which it exists and the way it influences a person's behavior. If there's a real cannibal culture where one person or department is going to lose power or stature when another does better, it can be very discouraging. The level of politics also rises correspondingly. Just look at recent headlines in the business section to see what greed can do to people.

Where Did My Life Go?

Asset management is less demanding than I-banking or management consulting, but you're still going to have to work hard for your money. You'll want to be at the office bright and early before the market opens to see what's happening in the *Wall Street Journal* and prepare for the day's action. If you work in California, expect to roll in bright and early at 5:00 a.m. "The biggest downside is that the job never ends," says one insider. "Even when you're on vacation, the market is running. I call on the traders a few times a day to make sure positions don't blow up."

International fund managers are particularly hard-pressed, because so much of their business is conducted overseas. That can mean long trips and meetings scheduled according to Singapore time. If you're an analyst or manager, there's always one more thing you should read, one more fact to know. That can be tough on people who don't know how to call it quits.

Unstable Ground

Merger activity among financial firms has been frantic in the past few years. Both in the United States and in other countries, all types of consolidations, purchases, and takeovers are changing the makeup of financial institutions, including mutual funds. Many mergers today are based on cost savings, and that means job cutting. So along with market volatility, these activities increase the pink-slip factor.

Slow to Change

Investment companies often have difficulty changing processes and procedures. Perhaps this is because companies must strive so hard to create a sense of stability in the midst of constantly changing markets. Insiders report some mutual fund companies have also had an ongoing problem integrating new technology—spending hundreds of millions of dollars on systems that have become part of an unmanageable patchwork of computers.

Getting Hired

Requirements

The Recruiting Process

Interviewing Tips

Getting Grilled

Grilling Your Interviewer

Requirements

Undergraduates with their hearts set on a career in asset management should take as many statistics and accounting classes as possible to prove that they can handle all of the number crunching and financial modeling that the profession requires. Undergraduates may be able to land jobs as research analysts, though competition is tough and they may be going up against candidates with MBAs.

If you're really serious about the profession, start with a job in sales, marketing, operations, or trading at an asset management firm, then consider going back for an MBA or taking your CFA before switching into asset management per se. You may also consider a 2-year analyst or research position in investment banking. Such jobs are more plentiful and provide excellent training for asset management.

Generally, MBAs come aboard as researchers or analysts. Analysts and researchers generally serve at least 2 years before they come up for consideration as fund managers. It's important to note, however, that not all asset management firms see the MBA as a key to success. The degree "is not that important for portfolio management," says one insider. "If you want to become a manager and run a marketing program, then perhaps it's useful. The CFA is the designation given the most reverence in asset management."

You are more likely to get an asset manager position earlier if you run smaller portfolios for institutional asset managers or private banks that offer services to the wealthy. On the mutual fund side, you might become portfolio comanager, sharing the management responsibility with a senior manager. The larger the pool of assets, the fiercer the competition.

There is no single prerequisite to becoming an asset manager. It all comes down to how much money you can make with other people's money. That said, virtually all successful asset managers possess the following skills.

QUANTITATIVE AND ANALYTICAL SKILLS

Asset managers have to be able to read spreadsheets and earnings reports. And they have to be able to take those numbers and crunch them into financial models and future projections. Even if you're dealing with less volatile investments such as bonds or real estate, you have to do the math to stay ahead of conventional wisdom. Classes in accounting and statistics are a big help, as are jobs that require number crunching, from I-banking to management consulting.

MANAGERIAL AND ORGANIZATIONAL SKILLS

Whether you're a researcher or a fund manager, you'll have to keep track of reams of facts to glean the really important information. Furthermore, you'll have to be able to make decisions—and execute them—quickly and accurately. Delay can cost big money. Finally, you need to be able to motivate and manage a talented staff of researchers and analysts if you work your way up to portfolio manager. Without their coordinated efforts, you may not have the information you need to make the best decision possible. "Solid general management experience is always in demand," says a recruiter. "There is such an opportunity for financial success without managing people at all that many professionals don't do it, don't want it, and don't develop the skills."

PROFESSIONAL LICENSING

In general, asset managers who work behind the scenes and make the big decisions don't need professional licensing. But if you're dealing with the public at all, you probably will, especially if you're in a position to make buy and sell recommendations directly to a client. For example, you may need a NASD license (Series 7, 63, or 65), or certain insurance licenses. Employers will generally give you the time to get such licenses once you're hired and may even pay the costs.

The Recruiting Process

Barclays Capital, Merrill Lynch, Deutsche Bank, Credit Suisse, and Vanguard are among the many diverse asset management companies and brokerage firms that recruit on campus. It can really pay off to interview with several of the major firms, but you should also dig up a few smaller alternatives where you might get on a faster track to more responsibility with much less structure. If a company you've got your sights on doesn't recruit on campus, which often happens if no alums are working at the firm, it's best to know someone. "You have to have friends in the industry who can make sure they look at your resume."

UNDERGRADUATES

Undergraduates from all disciplines are hired into asset management companies. The best option is to check job listings and company websites and contact the company directly. If you can impress on a mutual fund recruiter that you value the customer and can be trained to use the computer system to access account and market information, you can start in a sales capacity and get a basic understanding of the business by training on the job. From there you can talk to people in other departments to find additional areas of interest.

MBAS

If your goal is to manage money, you need to select asset management companies you think you might want to work for and start networking. The selection process for portfolio managers is formal and very competitive. It's less formal but still selective for other positions. You need to find out what particular qualities a company is looking for. The more you understand a particular company's investment philosophy and can discuss it intelligently while networking and interviewing, the more likely the company will take an interest in you as a potential hire. There is some campus recruitment for portfolio managers, analysts, and researchers, but the companies also hire through local advertisements and headhunters. Strong academic credentials and demonstrated market knowledge are musts.

MIDCAREER CANDIDATES

Midcareer professionals can reap big returns in sales positions and may be prime candidates for retail brokerage training programs. For these jobs, you will have to go through the rigmarole of getting a Series 7 license—not a cakewalk, but not the bar exam either. A marketing background is easily transferable into a marketing position in the financial industry. Check job listings, search company websites, and make direct contact with the firms of your choice to get your foot in the interviewer's door.

Interviewing Tips

Though the stock market posted terrific gains in 2003 and in parts of 2004, hiring has yet to keep pace with the market; recruiting is picking up, but competition for top-shelf jobs is still fierce. Research your potential candidates well and follow these tips:

1. The asset management industry loves teamwork. You'll make a better impression if you talk about your values, your work ethic, and the importance of teamwork rather than your love of the spotlight.

2. Different firms in different cities all have their own distinctive character and style. Research the culture and be able to articulate how you'll fit in.

3. For portfolio managers, analysts, and researchers, be conversant in investment theories and models such as CAPM (capital asset pricing model) and *Graham and Dodd's Security Analysis*, the classic textbook on value investing. Discuss industries where you have specific knowledge. Reveal your best stock picks and your dream portfolio.

4. Be yourself, but be direct. Be able to communicate your work experience and educational highlights in 30- or 60-second sound bites. This is a valued skill in an industry where the ability to summarize information quickly and accurately is so important.

5. Remember that behind all of the charts and graphs there is an investor, the customer. Let your interviewer know that you understand how important that person is.

6. The investment industry is, after all the research and analysis is done, about opinions. Both for retail brokers and research analysts, presenting an aura of confidence and authority is critical for success.

Getting Grilled

While the investment industry is vast and job functions vary greatly, the following will give you some idea of the range of questions that interviewers commonly ask. Those in the "Rare" section are innocuous, while the "Well Done" questions will prove more difficult to answer.

RARE

- What are your greatest strengths?

- What are your greatest weaknesses?

- What role do you play in team projects?

- Where do you want to be in 5 years?

- What accomplishment are you most proud of?

- Why do you want to work at [company name]?

- What about the industry interests you?

- How do you like to spend your free time?

MEDIUM

- Tell me about a stock you would recommend.

- How do you keep informed about the financial markets?

- How would you value Company X?

- What are the primary differences in valuing companies in Industry X versus Industry Y?

- What sectors do you like now?

- Describe your ideal job.

- What stocks are you following?

WELL DONE

- Why should we hire you?

- Why are you interested in asset management instead of investment banking?

- Tell me about a time you failed.

- Give me an example of a time when one of your investment decisions failed? How did you handle it?

- What political and economic factors are affecting financial markets?

- How do you see our firm as we relate to competitors?

- What will happen to bond prices if interest rates fall/rise?

- How do you know you can sell?

Grilling Your Interviewer

This is your chance to turn the tables and find out what you really want to know about the asset management and retail brokerage industry. The following generic questions will fit most industry interviews, but you'll no doubt want to come up with a few of your own. Those in the "Rare" section are meant to be innocuous, while the "Well Done" questions will put fire under your interviewer's feet.

RARE

- What is the company culture like? What kinds of people do well here?

- Is there a career path or formal channel of advancement?

- What is the bonus structure, and what is the company's history of paying bonuses?

- Is it difficult to transfer to other departments in the company?

MEDIUM

- What new developments do you see in the next year and beyond?

- What training and educational options do you offer and pay for?

- Do you stick to one investment philosophy?

- Can I trade my own account?

WELL DONE

- Do you monitor or record telephone conversations with clients?

- Is there any bias you've observed in the promotional process?

- Are there any unwritten rules?

- What do you think of Alan Greenspan?

For Your Reference

Industry Lingo

Articles

Books

Online References

Industry Lingo

The following terms are common to the brokerage and asset management industries. Based on our interviews with insiders, we selected terms that are appropriate to these industries, as well as those that are critical to an understanding of the broader financial services industry. See the "Online Glossaries" section for a list of additional resources you can look to for any industry terms not included here.

10-K. Annual report required of public companies by the SEC. The 10-K contains more detailed financial information and descriptions of a company's business and business risk than does the glossy, but comparatively Milquetoast, annual report. Foreign companies file annual reports that are submitted as forms 20-F.

10-Q. Quarterly report required of public firms by the SEC.

12B-1 fees. Fees collected by some mutual funds based on a percentage of assets and share price.

401(k). A plan offered by a corporation to individuals to allow them to save for retirement.

Advisor. A person or company responsible for investing fund assets.

Active investment. An investment by a fund manager that seeks to outperform market indices.

Alpha. The coefficient of risk-adjusted performance for a security, rather than volatility compared to the overall market (beta). Alpha is used to measure absolute performance and is beginning to become a popular measure of mutual fund performance, as it offers a measure of performance compared to an unmanaged portfolio of the same risk level (beta). Portfolios with a positive alpha are performing better than unmanaged portfolios; those with negative alphas are performing worse.

Arbitrage. The practice of opportunistically taking advantage of price differentials among securities to profit from market inefficiencies.

Asset. Any item with economic value owned by an individual that can be sold for cash.

Back office. The operations of a brokerage that process and report transactions. Many asset management companies concentrate on investing and outsource back-office operations to companies like State Street.

Bar. Industry parlance for a million units of currency.

Beta. The measure of volatility of a stock in comparison to the general market. A stock with a beta of 1 will have the same volatility as the market. A stock with a beta greater than 1, such as a biotech start-up, will have greater volatility—sort of a manic-depressive personality with higher highs and lower lows. A sleepy old dog of a stock like a utility might have a beta of less than 1 and therefore less volatility than the overall market.

Bid. The price a buyer is willing to pay for a security.

Block trade. The sale or purchase of a large number of shares of a security.

Buy-side analyst. A securities analyst who is employed by an asset management firm, mutual fund, or similar entity that invests in its own accounts. Unlike sell-side analysts, buy-side analysts cover multiple firms within multiple industries.

Call option. The option to purchase a security at a set price in the future.

Capital market. Market where companies and governments go to raise capital through the sale of medium- and long-range securities.

Chartered Financial Analyst (CFA). An industry credential administered by CFA Institute (formerly the AIMR), a nonprofit association of more than 75,000 investment professionals from 117 countries. The CFA credential requires at least 3 years of professional investment experience, successful completion of three 6-hour tests over 2 years, and commitment to an ethical code of conduct.

Chinese wall. A procedure in a brokerage firm put in place to keep groups that have insider or market-sensitive information from sharing that information outside the group.

Closed-end fund. A mutual fund with a fixed number of shares that is often traded on an exchange.

Dealer. A person or company buying securities for their own account.

Derivative. Any financial instrument whose value is derived from an underlying asset such as a stock, bond, currency, market, or market index. For instance, a call or *put option* (see entry following) on a stock is a derivative.

Desk. A department in a brokerage firm or asset management company that trades a particular type of security. For instance, a trader may be on the high-yield desk or the options desk.

Equity. Describes any security that has an ownership interest in a company, most often a stock.

Expense ratio. Metric that measures the costs associated with managing and running a fund.

Feeder fund. Similar to a fund of funds, a feeder fund does all of its business through other funds. It is often used to give domestic investors the tax advantages of investing in foreign funds.

Fixed-income security. Any security that pays a set interest rate, including bonds, money market instruments, and preferred stock.

Front loaded mutual fund. A fund in which management fees are paid at the time of purchase.

Fund of funds. A fund that invests in other funds. Funds of funds are especially popular in the hedge fund world, where the fund of fund manager can manage risk by taking advantage of the investment styles of many different hedge fund managers.

Fundamental analysis. Market analysis based on macroeconomic factors such as large-scale supply and demand, as well as a company's financial statements.

Hedge fund. A fund that is less regulated by the SEC and therefore can use instruments that are unavailable to mutual funds and traditional funds such as use of program trading, derivatives, short positions, leverage, and arbitrage. Hedge funds are said to be uncorrelated to market movements.

High-yield security. A below investment grade security, also known as a *junk bond*, which offers the buyer a high yield in exchange for increased risk.

Index fund. A mutual fund whose portfolio is composed of the same proportions as a major stock index.

Institutional investor. An investor or company that invests on behalf of another organization, such as an insurance company or pension fund.

Leverage. The use of borrowed money to purchase securities. Hedge funds often use leverage as an investment tool.

Load fund. A fund whose shares are sold with a large fee at the time of purchase or redemption of shares.

Offer. The price at which a seller is willing to sell a security.

Over the counter (OTC). An informal market set up by dealers to trade securities not listed on major exchanges.

Passive investment. An investment, such as an index fund, that seeks to mirror performance of a market index by constructing a portfolio that mirrors that of the index.

Payout. The percentage of a customer commission or service fee that a retail stockbroker receives. Stockbrokers with major brokerage firms receive around 40 percent, whereas independent brokers receive substantially higher rates, up to nearly 100 percent, but might have to pay for their own offices, assistants, and transaction processing fees.

Pension. Compensation an employee receives after he or she has retired.

Portfolio. The composition of a fund, which may contain any combination of stocks, bonds, and money market investments.

Portfolio trade. A trade in which a portfolio manager sells a number of different portfolio stocks to rebalance the portfolio.

Primary market. The market in which securities are initially offered to buyers, for instance an IPO or a debt issuance.

Prime broker. A broker that settles trades and provides custody services for a client as well as loans securities and provides loans. Hedge funds are big clients of prime brokers such as Goldman Sachs.

Program trading. Automated trading based on computer models that take advantage of price discrepancies between markets and securities.

Put option. The option to sell a security at a given price in the future.

Secondary market. The market for securities after initial distribution.

Security. Any financial instrument that shows evidence of ownership of a stock or bond.

Sell-side analyst. A securities analyst employed by an investment bank, brokerage firm, or independent company who researches and recommends securities, usually within a single industry.

Series 7. License required to sell all types of securities and therefore to be a stockbroker or financial advisor. The Series 7 is the SAT of the financial services industry. The test runs 6 hours and consists of 250 questions covering debt and equities securities, options and derivatives, securities regulation, retirement plans, investment companies, taxation, and financial analysis. Many brokerage firms will pay for training for their employees.

Series 63. State required license to become a stockbroker. Not all states require a Series 63 license.

Stockbroker. A person who buys and sells stocks on behalf of a client.

Taft-Hartley plan. A multiemployer pension plan established under the sweeping labor legislation of 1947 known as the Taft-Hartley Act. A Taft-Hartley plan allows workers to gain credit for pensions while working for many different employers, as defined by collective bargaining agreements. Essentially a labor union fund. The Teamsters' pension plans are governed by Taft-Hartley legislation.

Technical analysis. Analysis based purely on historical stock and market price data.

Trader. A person who buys and sells securities for his or her own account.

Wirehouse. A large, national brokerage firm (named so because wirehouse firms used to be connected to one another electronically), as opposed to an independent brokerage.

Yield curve. The relationship between short-term and long-term interest rates, expressed graphically. The X-axis represents the maturation term, with short-term rates on the left and longer terms toward the right. The Y-axis denotes the interest rate.

Articles

"The Busiest Broker on Earth"

Fidelity Investments stealthily ramps up its online brokerage to pressure rivals Charles Schwab and Merrill Lynch.

Aaron Pressman, *BusinessWeek*, April 7, 2005.

"Northern Trust's New Wanderlust"

The Midwestern wealth manager does its Grand Tour.

Adrienne Carter, *BusinessWeek*, April 11, 2005.

"Lazard's Clash of the Titans"

Details the power struggle between Lazard's French partners and brash American deal-maker Bruce Wasserstein leading up to the venerable investment bank's 2005 IPO.

Vicky Ward, *Vanity Fair*, April 2005.

"Wall Street on the Run"

Describes how Elliot Spitzer is single handedly changing the business model of sell-side analysts.

Andrew Nocera, *Fortune*, June 14, 2004.

"Eddie Stern's Passion"

A lurid insider tale of the mutual fund scandal.

Peter Elkind, *Fortune*, April 19, 2004.

"The House Always Wins"

Gary Pilgrim turns his fund into a money machine for himself.

John Helyar, *Fortune*, **March 8, 2004.**

"Are Hedge Funds Too Good To Be True?"

Describes the lure of hedge funds and the lack of regulation surrounding them.

Faith Arner, *BusinessWeek*, **May 10, 2004.**

"Can Sallie Save Citi?"

Thirty-eight-year-old Sallie Krawcheck is named CEO of Smith Barney. The article outlines issues facing the retail brokerage industry as well as gives a profile of the ex–Sanford C. Bernstein analyst.

David Rynecki, *Fortune*, **May 27, 2003.**

"Wall Street's Secret Power Elite: Where the Money is Really Made"

A summary of the current state of the hedge fund industry.

Andy Serwer, *Fortune*, **March 17, 2003.**

Books

Beating the Street

Peter Lynch (Fireside, 1994)

The author, Peter Lynch, beat the Street more consistently than most managers and propelled Magellan to international fame and fortune.

Buffett

Roger Lowenstein (Main Street Books/Doubleday, 1995)

A biography of legendary value investor Warren Buffett.

Fidelity's World:
The Secret Life and Public Power of the Mutual Fund Giant

Diana B. Henriques (Scribner, 1995)

An outsider's look at Fidelity, by a *New York Times* reporter whom management wouldn't talk to.

The Intelligent Investor: A Book of Practical Counsel

Benjamin Graham (HarperCollins, 4th rev ed, 1985)

Originally published in 1949, Graham's book has remained the most respected guide to investing due to his timeless philosophy of "value investing."

The Vanguard Experiment:
John Bogle's Quest to Transform the Mutual Fund Industry

Robert Slater (McGraw-Hill Trade, 1996)

Structured as a not-for-profit entity, John Bogle's company attracts some of the brightest talent around. Vanguard popularized the investment index.

Liar's Poker: Rising Through the Wreckage on Wall Street

Michael Lewis (Penguin USA, 1990)

Wall Street is one big game, and this hilarious and irreverent look at what it's really like to play in it is a must-read for all those who aspire to be players themselves.

The Mutual Fund Business

Robert C. Pozen and Sandra D. Crane (MIT Press, 1998)

The first textbook devoted exclusively to the mutual fund industry.

The Morningstar Approach to Investing

Andrew Lecky (Warner Books, 1997)

This respected mutual fund research organization gives a detailed look at funds and their managers.

Reminiscences of a Stock Operator

Edwin LeFevre (John Wiley & Sons, 1994)

Originally published in 1923, Reminiscences is the biography of Jesse Livermore, one of the greatest speculators of all time. Traders of all stripes consider this one of the all-time best accounts of trading life.

Securities Analysis

Benjamin Graham and David L. Dodd (McGraw-Hill, 1996)

The definitive text on value investing written by Warren Buffet's mentor. Graham and Dodd wrote the book in 1934, after the bubble had burst. Their approach to investing is deeply colored by this bust. Note that this 725-page monster is somewhat difficult to read for those without some understanding of accounting.

Valuation: Measuring and Managing the Value of Companies

Tom Copeland, Tim Koller, and Jack Murrin (John Wiley & Sons, 2000)
McKinsey's take on valuation techniques, a good primer on valuing companies for budding analysts.

When Genius Failed:
The Rise and Fall of Long-Term Capital Management

Roger Lowenstein (Random House, 2001)
A look inside one of the most famous and infamous hedge funds of all time and one that had on its staff none other than Nobel Prize–winning economist and inventor of the Black-Scholes model, Myron Scholes. The book gives insight not only into how hedge funds work, but the culture within them.

Online References

Investment Company Institute (www.ici.org)

An association of mutual fund companies. The site offers information about the organization of mutual funds, a mutual fund handbook, as well as copious statistics about the mutual fund industry.

The Investorside Research Association (www.investorside.org)

An association of independent research firms.

Pensions and Investments (www.pionline.com)

Pensions and Investments magazine's online presence. Contains industry news and statistics.

Institutional Investor (www.institutionalinvestor.com)

A subscriber site for the institutional investor community, with some free content, including news.

The Hedge Fund Association (www.thehfa.org)

Loose hedge fund industry association. It has some information about member companies and hedge fund investment strategies.

National Association of Securities Dealers (www.nasd.com)

Contains resources, glossaries, and investment information from the NASD, the self-regulating organization for the securities industry.

NASD Regulation page (www.nasdr.com)

Contains information on all the examinations (Series 7, etc.) administered by the NASD.

New York Stock Exchange (www.nyse.com)

The NYSE has a number of good resources that provide a background on how the market works and the anatomy of a trade.

ONLINE GLOSSARIES

General Terms

www.investorwords.com: a general glossary of financial terms

Brokerage and Trading Terms

www.nasd.com/web/idcplg?IdcService=SS_GET_PAGE&nodeId=766: NASD glossary

www.trading-glossary.com: glossary of trading terms sponsored by the Highlight Investments Group

Hedge Fund Terms

www.russell.com/II/Research_and_Resources/Alternative_Investing/Hedge_Fund_ Glossary.asp: Russell Institutional Investors' hedge fund glossary—full of arcane hedge fund terms

Mutual Fund Terms

www.investopedia.com/categories/mutualfunds.asp: glossary of mutual funds terms

WETFEET'S INSIDER GUIDE SERIES

Job Search Guides

Getting Your Ideal Internship

Job Hunting A to Z: Landing the Job You Want

Killer Consulting Resumes!

Killer Cover Letters & Resumes!

Killer Investment Banking Resumes!

Negotiating Your Salary & Perks

Networking Works!

Interview Guides

Ace Your Case: Consulting Interviews

Ace Your Case II: 15 More Consulting Cases

Ace Your Case III: Practice Makes Perfect

Ace Your Case IV: The Latest & Greatest

Ace Your Case V: Return to the Case Interview

Ace Your Interview!

Beat the Street: Investment Banking Interviews

Beat the Street II: I-Banking Interview Practice Guide

Career & Industry Guides

Careers in Accounting

Careers in Advertising & Public Relations

Careers in Asset Management & Retail Brokerage

Careers in Biotech & Pharmaceuticals

Careers in Brand Management

Careers in Consumer Products

Careers in Entertainment & Sports

Careers in Health Care

Careers in Human Resources

Careers in Information Technology

Careers in Investment Banking

Careers in Management Consulting

Careers in Marketing & Market Research

Careers in Nonprofits & Government Agencies

Careers in Real Estate

Careers in Retail

Careers in Supply Chain Management

Careers in Venture Capital

Industries & Careers for MBAs

Industries & Careers for Undergrads

Specialized Consulting Careers: Health Care, Human Resources, and Information Technology

Company Guides

25 Top Consulting Firms

25 Top Financial Services Firms

Accenture

Bain & Company

Booz Allen Hamilton

Boston Consulting Group

Credit Suisse First Boston

Deloitte Consulting

The Goldman Sachs Group

J.P. Morgan Chase & Co.

Lehman Brothers

McKinsey & Company

Merrill Lynch & Co.

Morgan Stanley

UBS

WetFeet in the City Guides

Job Hunting in New York City

Job Hunting in San Francisco